Wealth, Poverty, and Politics

Wealth, Poverty, and Politics

Gordon Tullock

Basil Blackwell

1566087

Library of Congress Cataloging in Publication Data

Tullock, Gordon.
   Wealth, poverty, and politics / Gordon Tullock.
      p.   cm.
   Includes index.
   ISBN 0–631–15113–3 : $50.00
   1. Social choice.   2. Income distribution.   3. Transfer payments
   4. Voting.   5. Decision-making.   I. Title.
   HB846.8.T84 1988
   302'.13—dc 19

British Library Cataloguing in Publication Data

   Tullock, Gordon.
      Wealth, poverty, and politics.
      1. Social choice   2. Political science
      3. Welfare economics
      I. Title
      320'.01'9   JA77

      ISBN 0–631–15113–3

Typeset in 11/13pt Sabon by Hope Services, Abingdon, Oxon
Printed in the USA by Maple Vail

Contents

Acknowledgments

The author and publisher are grateful to the following for kind permission to reproduce the articles in this book:
"Problems of Majority Voting," *Journal of Political Economy* 67 (December 1959), pp. 571–79, "In Defense of Majority Voting," *Journal of Political Economy* (February, 1961), pp. 192–199, and "Reply to a Traditionalist," *Journal of Political Economy* 69 (April 1961), pp. 200–03. © University of Chicago Press. "An Economic Analysis of Political Choice," *Il Politico* 16 (1961), pp. 234–40, © Università di Pavia. "Entry Barriers in Politics," *American Economic Review* 55 (May 1965), pp. 458–66, © American Economic Association. "The General Irrelevance of the General Impossibility Theorem," *Quarterly Journal of Economics* 81 (May 1967), pp. 256–70, © John Wiley. "Social Cost and Government Action," *American Economic Review* 59 (May 1969), pp. 189–97 and "A Simple Algebraic Logrolling Model," *American Economic Review* 60 (June 1970), pp. 419–26, © American Economic Association. "The Social Cost of Reducing Social Cost," in Garrett Hardin and John Baden (eds.), *Managing the Commons* (San Francisco: W. H. Freeman & Co., 1976), pp. 147–56. "Why So Much Stability?" *Public Choice*, Vol. 37, No. 2 (1981), pp. 189–202. "The Short Way With Dissenters," in Wolfgang Sodeur (ed.), *Okonomische Erklarungen Sozialen Verhaltens* vom 11–13, (Wuppertal, W. Germany, Marz 1982), pp. 201–23. "Income Testing and Politics: A Theoretical Model," in Irwin Garfinckel (ed.), *Income-Tested Transfer Programs: The Case For and Against* (New York: Academic Press, 1982), pp. 97–116. "A (Partial) Rehabilitation of the Public Interest

Theory," *Public Choice* Vol. 42, No. 1 (1984), pp. 89–99. "How To Do Well While Doing Good!" Reprinted with permission from David C. Colander (ed.), *Neoclassical Political Economy: The Analysis of Rent-seeking and DUP Activities* (Copyright 1984, Cambridge, MA: Ballinger Publishing Company) pp. 229–39.

Introduction

Public Choice is, essentially, an invasion of political science by the economists. Most of the pioneers were economists by training, although William Riker is, of course, an outstanding exception, being someone who was not originally an economist.

My basic training was in law, and while in law school I received a one-quarter course in economics taught by Henry Simons. It had an immense effect on my life. I began reading the main economic journals (which were easier to read in those days) from cover to cover, although I still remained primarily interested in law and politics. Indeed, I joined the Department of State and intended to make a career as a political officer there. It was a general dissatisfaction with what I read in political science that led me to feel that a completely new approach was necessary. Oddly, this decision was made in Communist China. I was left in China with the rest of the American Diplomatic establishment when the Communists took over the country, because the Department of State was planning on recognizing the new government. The Communists cut off our communications but did nothing very much to interfere with our daily life. As a result, I found myself with a great deal of leisure time on my hands and a reasonably good basic library provided by the USIS readily available. My reading of the political science literature convinced me that something better was needed.

When I came back from China, I was sent to Yale and Cornell universities to study Chinese and related subjects and one day, in the Yale co-op, I saw a big pile of red-jacketed books, all entitled *Human Action: a Treatise on Economics* and written by a man I had never head of, Ludwig Von Mises. I bought a copy and read it. It was the first economics book that I had ever read all the way through, although by that time economics had become rather a hobby of mine.

The book had a great influence on me; I didn't realize at the time that it was presenting a special viewpoint rather then simply providing a foundation in economics. Having read it, I reread it, and, reading the methodological introduction for a second time, I suddenly realized how I could produce a theory of bureaucracies which would fit my experience in China and in the Department of State.

Since I was busily studying Chinese and was then employed by the Department of State in Hong Kong, Korea and finally Washington, I set aside serious work on this matter for several years. During that time I turned the idea over in my mind. When the Department of State and I finally came to the parting of the ways, I intended to write a book on bureaucracy and then start up an import and export business in the Far East. This was not to be.

My eventual swing into Academe was the result of two separate influences. First, I was for a while at New Haven, using the Yale library and working on a book, and there I met Richard Walker who invited me to join the Department of International Studies at the University of South Carolina.

An even more important event, however, occurred. I had had the manuscript of my book which eventually became *Politics of Bureaucracy* printed up in about 20 copies for the purpose of circulation to publishers. I also sent some to other places, including one to Warren Nutter whom I had known in the debating team at the University of Chicago. He was moving to the University of Virginia, where he and James Buchanan subsequently established the Thomas Jefferson Center for Political Economy and Social Philosophy. Buchanan and Leland Yeager read the book. I think Warren did not, although I have never been absolutely certain of that. In any event the three of them offered me a post-doctoral fellowship at the University of Virginia. Walker very tolerantly permitted me to take this up, even though it was to have been my first year at South Carolina.

My first year at Virginia as a Post-Doctoral Fellow was an extremely enlightening experience. I had never had a really good grounding in the foundations of economics and, in particular, did not myself approve of welfare economics. Buchanan changed both of these things.

I think that I had an equivalent impact on him and on Nutter. They really thought in terms of a rather modest expansion of economics along the lines of existing political economy. My totally different background and interests which were almost entirely in politics jarred them, in particular Buchanan, into adopting a much wider perspective. In any event the outcome was, of course, quite significant for the foundation of what we now call Public Choice.

Another important influence on me at that time was a book that I did not actually read: *The Affluent Society* by John Galbraith. Although I did not read the book itself, I did read the reviews and was highly irritated. I decided to write a proof that the government as well as private enterprise could overexpend, and the result was "Problems of Majority Voting," the acorn from which *The Calculus of Consent* grew.

While awaiting publication of "Problems of Majority Voting" I wrote two other monographs which were privately circulated among the very limited number of people who were in those days interested in the topic; they have not, up to the present, been formally published. The first of these was "A Preliminary Investigation of the Theory of Constitutions," another step in the development towards *The Calculus of Consent*; the other, "Entrepreneurial Politics," demonstrates that implicit logrolling produces much the same result as explicit logrolling.

I then went to South Carolina to take up my duties as Assistant Professor of International Studies. *The Calculus of Consent* was written by mail between Buchanan and myself; frankly, he doing most of the work from that point on.

"Problems of Majority Voting," of course, is reprinted in somewhat modified form in *The Calculus of Consent*. There is a significant difference between the two versions and it is not altogether clear which of them is better. The original version, reprinted in this volume, points out that presents to minorities in the form of tax exemption might be bought at the cost of reducing provision of public goods. This does not occur in *The Calculus of Consent* version because at the time that we were writing that book we were impressed by the possibility that with the progressive tax system there would always be overexpenditure. Retrospectively, looking at the matter from a 1988 standpoint instead of a 1962 one, I am not at all certain which of the two versions is closer to reality.

The article and the book were both regarded as quite revolutionary at the time and, interestingly enough, Anthony Downs, who in a way had been the first person to write a widely-circulated book in the field, was upset. The result was his criticism of "Problems of Majority Voting" and my response, both of which are reproduced in this volume. The paper that I wrote immediately after, "An Economic Analysis of Political Choice," was actually prepared to be read at the Southern Economic Association Meeting; once again Anthony Downs was the discussant, and was highly critical of the paper. Unfortunately, I have no copy of his comments or my reply to him.

This was, as far as I know, the first occasion in any learned society anywhere at which a panel discussed the topic of Public Choice. I regret to say that, other than the members of the panel, we had exactly two people in the audience.

This state of things changed with time and, in fact, a tradition developed that there would be a Public Choice panel at every Southern meeting. As a result, the theory of Public Choice was probably more widely known in the southern part of the United States than anywhere else in the first few years.

As another off-shoot of this matter, it would appear that *The Calculus of Consent* and the line of reasoning therein led to Anthony Downs's abandonment of Public Choice. There were, of course, other reasons: he became involved in his father's Real Estate Research Corporation and that took a great deal of his time. However, I do think that Tony is deeply and emotionally attached to simple majority voting as a way of making a decision and finds skepticism about it, which is a characteristic of Public Choice work, painful. In any event, he has written practically nothing in the field between the publication of *The Calculus of Consent* and the present. Currently, he is working on a general book on political theory which, interestingly, shows very little influence of Public Choice thought. In view of his pioneer status in the development of the theory of Public Choice, all of this is quite surprising.

"Entry Barriers in Politics" was an effort to get the subject of Public Choice into the American Economic Association as well as the Southern. It was, in fact, read at a meeting and published in their proceedings issue. The need for missionary activity can perhaps be illustrated by the fact that after the panel discussion, the chairman of the MIT Economics Department came up to me and said that he thought this was an interesting area and we should attempt to get more work done in it. It was clear that he had never heard of it before this paper.

Another mildly amusing aspect of this paper is that I accidentally anticipated Harold Demsetz's important work on natural monopolies. The suggestion that they be put up to bid is, of course, simply a stalking horse for the introduction of political methods. His latter, perfectly serious, suggestion of the same idea had a great effect on economics in this area.

The next article in this book, "The General Irrelevance of the General Impossibility Theorem," has had an intriguing history. When it was first published the Public Choice community was quite small, but the article had a significant impact on it. With time, the Public Choice community developed and a number of people conversant with high level mathematics moved into it. The article was first more or less forgotten and then subject to what was regarded by many people as disproof. The disproof was then itself "disproved," with the result that we have now practically returned to the position taken up in this article, although modern literature in the field is immensely more complicated. I suspect that this train of events reflects the fact that modern mathematical training gives much less emphasis to simple Euclidean geometry than the educational process that I went through.

In general, this work on general irrelevance deals with bills which are of wide public interest, i.e., genuine public goods (or bads). A large part of all government activity involves, of course, the passing of all sorts of minor specific provisions by logrolling. My realization that this theory of general irrelevance did not apply to that kind of work led to my more or less leaving the mathematical debate on the issue to the mathematicians rather than defending my position.

"The Social Costs of Reducing Social Cost" and "Social Cost and Government Action," are two articles on the desirable scope of government. The existing orthodoxy when Public Choice first entered the field held that when the market was imperfect we should turn to the government. The Public Choice point of view is that we only turn to the government if there is reason to believe that the government will be less imperfect than the market. When the article was first written, this was a new and more or less revolutionary idea. These two articles are part of the attack on the then conventional wisdom.

The "Simple Albegraic Logrolling Model" was just that: a simple way of handling logrolling with the Cartesian apparatus. I had forgotten my high school course in analytical geometry and on one occasion couldn't remember how one moved ellipses around, changed their shape, and so forth. I went over to the library and, being careful that nobody saw me, looked up some high school math texts. Unfortunately, it turned out that they were of no great use. High school use of the Cartesian mechanism apparently has changed since I was in high school and they no longer tell you how to fiddle with ellipses, but have you prove theorems in connection with them. Thus, I had to re-invent the thing myself. Even though I did re-invent it I have to admit that the mechanism is rather old-fashioned from the standpoint of modern mathematics.

I wrote "Why So Much Stability?" in an effort to answer the question of why there is so much stability in government action in spite of the fact that these large collections of bills appear to be theoretically unstable; I hoped at the same time to initiate discussion with other people on the subject. In my opinion the solution to the problem that I gave is a correct one, but I should say that most of the people who have written afterwards have rejected it and offered their own solution. Since they have offered very many mutually inconsistent solutions, I feel free to stick to my original idea. I should warn the reader that this particular article has been subject to a great deal of criticism.

"The Short Way with Dissenters" is a sample of my work on revolution, guerilla wars, and their possible repression. It is characteristic of the present-day world, that the really nasty governments, such as the government of North Korea, have no difficulty with rioting in their streets. South Korea, an infinitely better government even if not a perfect democracy, on the other hand, does have that problem. Indeed, all the Western European democracies have had more trouble with rioting by opposition groups than any Communist country. The article attempts to explain why, and also offers a method of dealing with such problems that, if not in complete accord with our traditional methods, in any event does not involve torture or censorship.

"Income Testing and Politics" is a sample of my work on income redistribution. Interestingly, here again my commentator was Anthony Downs, who obviously didn't like the paper, but was unable to break its logic. In his comment he added another variable to the ones I had been given by the sponsors of the conference at which the article had been presented. Using this other variable he reached a different conclusion. As it happens it was fairly easy to add the other variable and re-reach my conclusion.

This leaves us with two articles, both rather optimistic. "A (Partial) Rehabilitation of the Public Interest Theory" is just what it says. It indicates that, to some extent, considerations of public interest do influence politics. This does not contradict Public Choice work but does rather change the emphasis. The final article is the most optimistic of all. It points out that economists and Public Choice scholars can both improve their position in their academic institutions by publication and at the same time enjoy a feeling of moral justification by actually improving society.

In a way, this book is an intellectual autobiography. The reader will get a pretty firm grasp of the ideas in which I have been interested and my approaches to them. It is not, of course, comprehensive. There is nothing here at all reflecting my work on biology; my one-page article on physics (Rhigodynamics) has obviously been left out; and my work on economics and the law is completely ignored. These articles do, however, cover the areas where I have been most influential and where my work is best known.

Marriageable girls used to produce things called samplers, examples of various forms of knitting and needlework designed to be framed and hung up in the parlor where potential swains could see them and judge the skill of the potential housewife. I am not of marriageable age, and even if I were I doubt whether any readers of this book would be interested. Nevertheless, in a real sense this book is a sampler of my work.

1

Majority Voting

I Problems of Majority Voting

Economists have devoted a great deal of thought to problems of governmental policy and, in particular, to the question of proper allocation of resources between the public and private sectors.[1] On the other hand, little attention has been given to the actual process of decision-making or to the type of policy likely to come out of the process.[2] It is the purpose of this article to discuss one particular method of making governmental decisions – majority voting – and to attempt to derive conclusions about its implications for resource allocation and government policy. It is hoped that the conclusions will be more realistic than current doctrine, which is based on an essentially economic view of what "ought" to happen.

Since it is impossible to talk about everything at once, the demonstration will be confined to certain features of the majority process. A number of other serious problems raised by the voting system will be disregarded. The most important of these concerns a series of difficulties and paradoxes in the voting process itself.[3] I will also disregard the fact that voters are frequently very poorly informed or even deceived in voting, the great oversimplification of issues necessary in order to reduce them to a form such that they can be determined by vote, and innumerable other possible limitations on the functional efficiency of the democratic process.

I shall consider the operation of majority rule under two different restrictions: logrolling (i.e., vote-trading) permitted and logrolling not permitted, starting with the latter. Since logrolling is the norm, discussion of the non-logrolling case must start with consideration of the institutional structure which eliminates logrolling. The standard referendum on a simple issue is the best example. The voter cannot trade his vote on one issue for votes on others because he and his acquaintances represent too small a part of the total electorate for this to be worth the effort involved. Further, the use of the secret ballot makes it impossible to tell whether voting promises are carried out. In these circumstances the voter will simply vote in accord with his preferences on each individual issue.

The contrary case, logrolling permitted, occurs under two circumstances. First, it occurs where a rather small body of voters vote openly on each measure; this is normally to be found in representative assemblies, but it may also be found in very small "direct democracy" units. Under these circumstances trades of votes are easy to arrange and observe and significantly affect the outcome. It is probable that this fact is one of the major reasons for the widespread use of representative democracy. The second type of logrolling, which may be called implicit logrolling, occurs when large bodies of voters are called on to decide complex issues, such as which party shall rule, or a complex set of issues presented as a unit for a referendum vote. Here there is no formal trading of votes, but an analogous process goes on. The "entrepreneurs" who offer candidates or programs to the voter make up a complex mix of policies to attact support.[4] In doing so, they keep firmly in mind the fact that the voter may be so interested in the outcome of some issue that he will vote for the party which supports it, although the party opposes him on other issues. This implicit logrolling will not be discussed further.

In the system in which logrolling is not permitted every voter simply indicates his preference, and the preference of the majority of the voters is carried out. The defect, and it is a serious one, of this procedure is that it ignores the various intensities of the desires of the voters. A man who is passionately opposed to a given measure and a man who does not much care but is slightly in favor of it are weighted equally. Obviously, both could very easily be made better off if the man who felt strongly were permitted to give a present to the man who had little preference in return for a reversal of his decision. The satisfaction of both would be improved, and the resulting situation would, on strictly Paretian grounds, be superior to the outcome of voting that weighed their votes equally. By way of illustration it is conceivable that a proposal to send all Negroes to Africa (or all Jews to Israel) would be passed by referendum. It would have not the slightest chance of passing Congress because the supporters of these two minorities would be willing to promise to support almost any other measure in return for votes against such a bill. In the absence of vote-trading, the support for it might reach 51 percent, but it would not be intense, at least in the marginal cases, and hence the trading process would insure its defeat.

Even voters who are more or less indifferent to a given issue may find their votes on it counting as much as those of the most highly concerned individuals. The fact that a voter votes normally proves that he is not completely indifferent, but many voters are motivated to vote on referendum issues more by a sense of duty to vote than by any real concern with the matter at hand. Under these circumstances even the tiniest preference for one side or the other may determine the issue. Permitting the citizens who feel very strongly about an issue to compensate those whose opinion is only feebly held can result in a great increase of the well-being of both groups, and prohibiting such transactions is to prohibit a movement toward the optimum surface.

Note that the result under logrolling and under non-logrolling differs only if the minority feels more intensely about the issue than the majority; if the feeling of the majority is equal to or more intense than the minority, then the majority would prevail both with and without logrolling. It is only when the intensity of feeling of the minority is sufficiently greater than that of the majority that they are willing to make sacrifices in other areas sufficient to detach the marginal voters from the majority (intense members of the majority might make counteroffers if they wished) that the logrolling process will change the outcome.

As an introduction to logrolling, let us consider a simple model. A township inhabited by 100 farmers who have more or less similar farms is cut by a number of main roads maintained by the state. However, these roads are limited-access roads, and the farmers are permitted to enter the primary network only at points where local roads intersect it. The local roads are built and maintained by the township. Maintenance is simple. Any farmer who wishes to have a specific road repaired puts the issue up to vote. If the repairing is approved, the cost is assessed to the farmers as part of the real property tax. The principal use of the local roads by the farmers is to get to and from the major state roads. Since these major roads cut through the district, generally there are only four or five farmers dependent on any particular bit of local road to reach the major roads.

Under these circumstances the referendum system would result in no local roads being repaired, since an overwhelming majority would vote against repairing any given road. The logrolling system, however, permits the roads to be kept in repair through bargains among voters. The bargaining might take a number of forms, but most of these would be unstable, and the "equilibrium" involves overinvestment of resources.

One form that the implicit bargain among the farmers might take is this: each individual might decide, in his own mind, the general standard that should be maintained. That is, he would balance, according to his own schedule of preferences, the costs of maintaining his own road at various levels of repair with the benefits to be received from it and reach a decision as to the point where the margins were equal. He could then generalize this decision: he could vote on each proposal to repair a given road in the same way as he would vote for repairs on his own road. If every voter followed this rule, we would find a schedule of voting behavior such as that illustrated in figure 1.1. Each mark on the horizontal line represents the standard of one voter for maintenance of all roads. If a proposal for repairing a given road falls to the left of his position, he would vote for it; if it falls to his right, against. If each road has at least one farmer whose preference for road repairs falls to the right of the median (*A* in figure 1.1) then a proposal for repairs would be made as soon as a given road fell below his preferred degree of repair and successive further such proposals as the road gradually deteriorated. When it reached the

Figure 1.1

median level, a repair proposal would pass; hence all roads would be repaired at the median preference.

Although this result would not be a Paretian optimum, it would be possible to argue for it in ethical terms. In fact, I believe that this is the result that most proponents of democracy in such situations have in the back of their minds. In any event, I intend to use this result, which I shall call "Kantian," as the "correct" result with which I shall contrast what actually happens. Since my Kantian result differs from the "equal marginal cost and marginal benefit" system used by most economists in this field, it is incumbent on me to explain why I use it. The reason is simple – it is the best I can do. I have been unable to find any system of voting which would lead to a social matching of costs and benefits at the margin.

If the farmers generally followed this policy in voting, then any individual farmer could benefit himself simply by voting against all proposals to repair roads other than his own and voting for proposals to repair his road at every opportunity. This would shift the median of the schedules slightly so that his taxes would be reduced or his road kept in better-than-average repair. If the other farmers on his road followed his example (we shall call farmers who follow this rule "maximizers"), they would be able to shift the standard of repair so that the roads on which they lived would be repaired at level B' while reducing the standard of repair on other roads to B. Since the largest share of the cost of keeping their road up falls on other taxpayers, while the largest share of their taxes goes for the repair of other roads, this change would be greatly to the advantage of the maximizers and greatly to the disadvantage of the Kantians.

If the farmers along another road also switched to a maximizing pattern, this would bring the level of road-repairing on the two maximizing roads down toward about that which would prevail under the Kantian system, while still further lowering the standards on the Kantian roads. However, it is likely that the two groups of maximizers could benefit by forming a coalition in order to raise the standards of road maintenance on their own roads. Let us consider the situation of an individual maximizer debating whether or not to enter such a coalition. Since he will pay only about 1/100th of the cost, practically any proposal to repair his own road is to his benefit. If, however, in order to obtain support for some repair project on his own road, he must also vote for the repair of another road, then he must also count the cost to him of this other repair project as part of the cost of his own road. In weighing the costs and benefits, he must consider not only the tax cost to himself of the repair of his own road but the tax cost of the other repair job which he must vote for in order to get his road done. In the particular case we are now discussing, when the farmers on all the roads except two are still Kantian, this would put few restraints on feasible projects, but it would still have to be considered. However, as more and more Kantians become tired of being exploited by the maximizers and switch to a maximizing pattern of behavior, this consideration would become more and more important.

Let us now examine a rather unlikely, but theoretically important, special case. Suppose that exactly 51 of our 100 farmers were maximizers, while 49 were Kantians. Further suppose that all the maximizers lived on some roads while all the Kantians lived on others. Under these circumstances the Kantians clearly would never get their roads repaired, but the level of repair on the maximizers' roads presents a more difficult problem. In order to simplify it, let us assume (plausibly) that they are maintained on a high enough level so that all the Kantians vote against any project for further repair. Under these circumstances it would be necessary to obtain the votes of all the maximizers for each repair project. A farmer considering whether he wants to have his road repaired must consider the whole cost, including the taxes he must pay in order to repair the roads of the other parties to the bargain. He can, however, simply compare his own marginal benefits and costs, and this requires no knowledge of anyone else's utility. He need only decide whether the total bargain is to his advantage or not.[5]

Note, however, that, while no roads leading to the Kantian farmers' houses will be repaired, they are required to contribute to the repair of the roads leading to the houses of the maximizers. Thus part of the cost of the road-repair projects will be paid by persons not party to the bargain, and, since the maximizers only count the costs to themselves of their votes, the general standard of road maintenance on the roads on which they live should be higher than if they had to count also the cost of maintaining the roads on which the Kantians lived. Under such conditions, where virtue so conspicuously is not paying, it seems likely that at least some of the Kantian farmers would decide to switch to a minimizing policy. For simplicity, let us assume that all of them do this at once. Since they would still be in a minority, their change of policy would not immediately benefit them, but surely they could find two of the original maximizers who would, in return for very good maintenance, desert their former colleagues. It is again obvious that the new majority would be susceptible to similar desertions; a permanent coalition of 51 farmers for the purpose of exploiting the remaining 49 could thus not be maintained. In terms of game theory any combination of 51 voters dominates any other size of combination, but no combination of 51 dominates all other combinations of 51.[6]

The outcome is clear. Each farmer would enter into bilateral agreements with enough farmers on other roads to insure that his own was repaired. He would then be forced to count as part of the cost of getting his road repaired the cost (to him) of repairing the roads of the other 50 farmers. These bilateral agreements, however, would overlap. Farmer A (more precisely the farmers on road A) would bargain with Farmers B, . . ., M. Farmer M, on the other hand, might make up his majority from Farmer A and Farmers N, . . ., Z.

Counting the cost to himself of the maintenance of his road in terms of support for other road-repair projects, each farmer would consider only those projects for which he voted. Thus his expenditure pattern would count the tax payments of 49 voters as a free gift. The natural result would be that each road would be maintained at a level considerably higher and at greater expense than is rational from the standpoint of the farmers living along it. Each individual behaves rationally, but the outcome is irrational. This apparent paradox may be explained as follows: each voter pays enough in support for repair of other roads to equalize the benefit he receives from the repair of his own road. But his payments counted under this system include only part of the road repair jobs undertaken.[7] There are others which are the result of bargains to which he is not a party. Taken as a group, the road-repair projects for which he votes represent a good bargain for him, but other *ad hoc* bargains to repair other roads will also take place. He will vote against these, but, as he will be in the minority, he will have to pay for them. The result is a sizable loss to him.

Any farmer following any other course of action will be even worse off. A Kantian farmer, for example, would never have his own road repaired but would pay heavy taxes for the support of repair jobs on other roads. The whole process will proceed through elaborate negotiations; the man who is the most effective bargainer will have a considerable advantage, but the general pattern will be less than optimal for all parties.

This seems a rather unsatisfactory result, and we should consider whether there are not ways of improving it. First, however, I should like to discuss certain possible objections to my reasoning.[8] It may be said that the maximizers are behaving wickedly and that ethical considerations will prevent the majority of the population from following such a course. Ethical systems vary greatly from culture to culture, and I do not wish to rule out the possible existence somewhere of an ethical system which could bar logrolling, but surely the American system does not. Under our system logrolling is normally publicly characterized as "bad," but no real stigma attaches to those who practice it. The press describes such deals without any apparent disapproval, and, in fact, all our political organizations bargain in this fashion.

A second argument asserts that each farmer in our community would realize that, if he adopted a maximizing policy, this would lead all other farmers to do the same. Since the "maximizing equilibrium" is worse for all[9] the farmers than the "Kantian median," each farmer would, on the basis of cold, selfish calculation, follow the Kantian system. This argument is similar to the view that no union will force its wage rate up because each union realizes that such action will lead other unions to do the same, the eventual outcome being higher prices and wage rates but no increase in real income. There seems to be overwhelming empirical evidence that men do not act this way; in addition, the argument contains a logical flaw. This is the observation that, in any series of actions by a number of men, there must be a first one. If this can be prevented, then the whole series can be prevented. This is true, of course, but there also must be a second, a third, etc. If any one of these is prevented, then the whole series cannot be carried out. If all our 100 farmers would refrain from a maximizing course of action because each one felt that his personal adoption of such a course would lead to a switch to the "maximizing equilibrium," then, if one of them had done so, we could construct an exactly similar argument "proving" that no 1 of the 99 remaining farmers would follow his example. But if this second argument is true, then the first is false; and hence the chain of reasoning contains an inconsistency.

I turn now to possible methods of improving the results. Could the members of a community somehow enter into an enforceable bargain under which they act according to the Kantian model? In the very narrow special case of our model, it is at least conceivable that they could. It is possible that a clear, unambiguous formula for telling when a road needed repair might be agreed upon, and then the exact figures to be inserted in the formula determined by general voting. Probably even in our case this would not be practical, but the theoretical possibility must be admitted.

In the more general and realistic case where governmental units deal with a continuing stream of radically different projects, no such agreed formula would be possible. A formula which would permit weighing such diverse programs as building giant irrigation projects in the West to increase farm production, paying large sums of money to farmers in the Midwest to reduce farm production, giving increased aid to Israel, and dredging Baltimore's harbor is inconceivable. There could not, therefore, be any agreement on an automatic system of allocating resources, and this throws us back to making individual decisions with the use of logrolling.

This is by no means a tragedy. If it were possible to set up some system by present voting to determine future resource allocation, it is more likely that this determination would take a form favored by a simple majority of the voters than a form favored by the whole group unanimously. This is likely to result in a worse decision than that resulting from logrolling. The problem of intensity must also be considered. The Kantian system makes no allowance for the differential intensities of the voters' preferences. If the voters who wanted more resources spent on road-repairing felt more intensely about it than the voters who wanted less, then the Kantian system would not result in an optimum distribution of resources. Permitting logrolling would take care of this problem.

Requiring more than a simple majority would reduce the resources spent on roads, since more people would have to be included in each bargain, and the cost to each voter of repair to this road would consequently be increased. The larger the majority required, the more closely would the result approach a Pareto optimum. Practically, however, the difficulty of negotiating a bargain would increase exponentially as the number of required parties increased, and this might make such a solution impossible. The provision in so many constitutions for a two-house legislature, each house elected according to a different system, raises much the same issues.

Our next problem is to inquire to what extent the results obtained in our simple model can be generalized. It would appear that any governmental activity which benefits a given individual or group of voters and which is paid for from general taxation could be fitted into our model. It is not necessary that the revenues used to pay for the projects be collected equally from all voters. All that is necessary is that the benefits be significantly more concentrated than the costs. This is a very weak restraint, and a very large number of budgetary patterns would fit it. If the taxes were collected by some indirect method so that individuals could not tell just how much they were paying for any given project, then this fact would accentuate the process. In the marginal case the individual might be indifferent about projects benefiting other people whose cost to him was slight and difficult to calculate.

One requirement of the process has not yet been emphasized. It is necessary that the voting on the various projects be a continuing process. A number of different projects or groups of projects must be voted on at different times. If all projects were inserted in a single bill to be accepted or rejected for all time, then 51 percent of the voters could fix the bill permanently to exploit the remainder. In fact, of course, since government is a continuing process, our condition is fulfilled.

The process which we have been discussing can be generalized to cover other types of government activity. We shall start by generalizing it to cover other types of taxation-expenditure problems and then turn to other types of governmental problems. First, let us suppose that we have some governmental activity of general benefit, police work, for example, which is paid for by some general type of taxation. By reasoning paralleling that which we have done so far, we can demonstrate that special tax exemptions to special groups at the expense of the general efficiency of the police force would be carried on to a degree which would far exceed the Kantian median. Similarly, if a given sum of money is to be spent on two different types of governmental activity, one of which is of general benefit and one of which benefits a series of special groups, too much will be spent on the latter. Defense, for example, will be slighted in favor of river and harbor work.

The same reasoning can be applied to the tax structure. If a given amount of money had to be raised, we would expect it to be raised by general taxes that were "too heavy" but riddled by special exemptions for all sorts of groups. This would greatly reduce the effect of any general tax policy, such as progression, that had been adopted. This pattern appears to be very realistic. On the basis of our theory, we would predict general and diffuse taxes, riddled with special exceptions, and governmental functions of general benefit sacrificed in favor of the interests of particular groups. I see no great conflict between the prediction and reality.

To apply our theory generally to all types of governmental activity, however, we must radically generalize it. For any individual voter all possible measures can be arranged according to the intensity of his feeling. His welfare can be improved if he accepts a decision against his desire in an area where his feelings are comparatively weak in return for a decision in his favor in an area where his feelings are strong. Bargains between voters, therefore, can be mutually beneficial. Logically, the voter should enter into such bargains until the marginal "cost" of voting for something he disapproves of but about which his feelings are weak exactly matches the marginal benefit of the vote on something else which he receives in return. Thus he will benefit from the total complex of issues which enter into the set of bargains which he makes with other people. In making these bargains, however, he must gain the assent of a majority of the voters only, not of all of them. On any given issue he can safely ignore the desires of 49 percent. This means that he can afford to "pay" more to people for voting for his measures because part of the inconvenience imposed by the measure will fall on parties not members of the bargains.

Unfortunately, the converse also applies. Bargains will be entered into in which our voter does not participate but part of the cost of which he will have to bear. As a result, the whole effect of the measures which result from his bargains and on which he votes on the winning side will be beneficial to him. But this will be only slightly more than half of all the "bargained" measures passed, and the remainder will be definitely contrary to his interest. The same would be true for the *average* voter under a pure referendum system. In fact, the whole problem discussed in this paper arises from the system of compelling the minority to accept the will of the majority.

Although this paper so far has been an exercise in "positive politics," the analysis does raise important policy problems, and at least some comment on them seems desirable. It seems clear that the system of majority voting is not by any means an optimal method of allocating resources. This fact should be taken into account in considering whether some aspect of our economy would be better handled by governmental or market techniques. On the other hand, these problems and difficulties do not materially reduce the advantage which voting procedures have over despotism as a system of government. The primary lesson would appear to be the need for further research. Majority voting plays the major role in the governments of all the nations in which the social sciences are comparatively advanced. It seems likely that careful analysis of the process would lead to the discovery of improved techniques and a possible increase in governmental efficiency.

II In Defense of Majority Voting

In a recent article entitled "Problems of Majority Voting," Gordon Tullock presented an ingenious model to illustrate certain problems which he believes arise from the use of simple majority voting in democracies.[10] It is my contention that the problems he describes are not caused by majority voting and that the generalizations he makes about the real world based on the model are not true, because real democracies do not use the form of voting he sets forth. Therefore, in this article I shall attempt to defend majority voting from Tullock's attacks, though this defense does not constitute a general rationalization of majority rule.

The basic premise behind simple majority rule is that every voter should have equal weight with every other voter. Hence, if disagreement occurs, it is better for more voters to tell fewer what to do than vice versa. The only practical arrangement to accomplish this is simple majority rule. Any rule requiring more than a simple majority for passage of an act allows a minority to prevent action by the majority, thus giving the vote of each member of the minority more weight than the vote of each member of the majority. For example, if a majority of two-thirds is required for passage, then opposition by 34 percent of the voters can prevent the other 66 percent from carrying out their desires. In effect, the opinion of each member of the 34 percent minority is weighted the same as the opinion of 1.94 members of the 66 percent majority. All rules of voting other than the majority rule have this same defect.

However, as Tullock points out, the equal weighting of all votes can lead to undesirable results when voters do not have equally intense preferences. If a minority passionately desires some act which the majority just barely opposes, there is no way for the minority to express its great intensity in a simple once-for-all vote, unless buying and selling of votes is allowed. However, when a series of issues is under consideration, expression of intensities can be allowed for by the trading of votes and promises of reciprocal support among voters. It is this possibility of "logrolling" to which Tullock devotes his model.

In the model, 100 farmers living on different roads are seeking to keep their roads repaired. Each road-repair action requires a separate vote by all the farmers, and the costs of each repair are spread evenly over all of them. If no vote-trading is allowed, every road-repair proposal will be defeated, since 99 farmers will gain nothing from it but have to bear some of the costs.[11] But, if farmers are allowed to trade promises of support, then each will seek to enter into agreements with at least 50 others so that he can insure that his road will be repaired in return for his supporting repair of their roads.

Remarkably enough, the result of this process is that every farmer finds himself paying more in taxes for the repairs of other roads than he gets for the repair of his own. He is financially a net loser from government action – but so is every other farmer. Hence the farmers as a group behave irrationally because they devote too many resources to repairing their roads; yet it is individually rational for them to do so.

Tullock reaches this conclusion via the following reasoning. In order to get his own road-repair bill passed, each farmer must obtain the support of 50 others, which he does by agreeing to support the road-repair bills of each of them. The amount of resources devoted to repairs in each such bill is arrived at by balancing the marginal cost against the marginal benefit. That is, each farmer weighs the amount he will receive when his own bill is passed against the total cost to him of supporting his bill and the fifty others. However, this cost is borne not only by the fifty-one farmers in the bargain but also by the forty-nine other farmers not in the bargain. Thus, he stands to gain about $1/51$st of the total cost for a payment of only $1/100$th of it. Assuming diminishing marginal utility of income and of road repairs, this means he is willing to request for himself – and support for others – a higher level of road repair than he would if he had to pay $1/51$st of the cost. He raises the level of road repair he is willing to support until he is in marginal equilibrium between gains from road repair and losses from taxes.

However, his calculation turns out to be in error. This occurs because the 50 farmers he has bargained with are also in similar bargains – but not all with each other. Instead, many of them have included in their bargains some of the 49 farmers not in his bargain and excluded some of the 50 in his bargain. A system of "revolving majorities" has sprung up because the 49 farmers who were left out when the first set of bills was passed have successfully offered excellent "deals" to some members of the majority bloc, wooing these members into supporting their bills too. Thus, as many as 100 road-repair bills will in fact be passed, although nearly every farmer individually is making calculations as though only the 51 bills he is supporting will be passed. Since he will have to pay 1/100th of all 100 bills (assuming 100 are passed), he comes out paying much more than he calculated, and he finds himself out of balance at the margin.

It might be argued that he will learn from this experience and lower the level of repair he will support, because he will guess that he will be forced to pay for 100 bills instead of just 51. But he will always seek to maximize the amount spent in his own repair bill, since the more he gets, the more likely he is to offset the unknown costs that will fall on him from others. Similarly, the other 50 men in his bargain are all seeking to maximize their own bills. If any one of them refuses to go along with the others, they will not support his high level of repairs. Thus, he is forced into continuing his support of large repairs, even though they make him a net loser. Only if he can create a permanent cartel out of 51 farmers can a lower level be enforced. However, in that case there is no reason to have lower levels, since the cartel can defeat all 49 other road-repaid bills. But such cartels cannot hang together because the 49 non-members can make such an outstanding offer to any two members of the cartel that they cannot rationally resist it. Thus no 51-farmer combination can dominate all others; so revolving majorities spring up, and overinvestment in road repairs inevitably results.

From this ingenious model Tullock expands to the following general conclusions:

1 Government activity which benefits minorities will receive disproportionate allocations of resources in comparison with that which benefits the citizenry as a whole.
2 Taxes of general impact will be riddled with exemptions favoring special groups.
3 The government budget as a whole will be too large, because each citizen will be driven by individual rationality to support a level of government spending which is irrational as a whole.

This makes almost every citizen a net financial loser to the government sector. Tullock believes these conclusions are applicable to the real world as well as his model. He states that the undesirable conditions they portray arise "from the system of compelling the minority to accept the will of the majority."

It is my contention that these conditions – even if they exist in the real world – are not the result of the majority principle at all. In order to prove this point, I must first examine the assumptions which underlie Tullock's model. The model is based upon the following premises:

1　Acts of legislation can discriminate between individuals regarding expenditures but not regarding taxation. That is, every tax must be levied upon all equally, but spending can be directed toward particular individuals only. This we shall call the *discrimination* assumption.

2　Acts of legislation are voted upon directly by the citizenry. This we shall call the *referendum* assumption.

3　The road-repair program is never considered as a whole but is broken into individual projects which are put to a vote one at a time. Thus, the voters face a continuing series of proposals spread over time, and the outcome of future votes is never known at the time of each present vote. We shall call this the *seriatim* assumption.

4　Voters can effectively bargain with each other and make viable promises of vote-trading. Following Tullock, we shall label this the *logrolling* assumption.

5　Each act proposed for a vote is carried if a majority supports it. This is the *majority* assumption.

6　A fairly large number of acts can be proposed and will actually be put to a vote. This we shall call the *multiple-activity* assumption.

7　Voting occurs on one and only one issue – road-repairing. We shall call this the *exclusiveness* assumption. (Tullock specifically relaxes this assumption before making his general conclusions.)

Once we have spelled out these assumptions, it is apparent that most of them are not applicable to real-world democracies and that the majority assumption is not the cause of the results of Tullock's model. Let us examine these two contentions in order.

Of the seven assumptions upon which Tullock's model is based, only two – the discrimination and majority assumptions – are actually operative in most real-world democracies.[12] Since most democratic societies use republican forms of government, the other assumptions simply do not apply. Citizens do not vote directly upon individual legislative acts; they do not vote on a continuing series of proposals but face periodic elections in which the government's entire program is considered as a whole; they do not bargain directly with each other; they cannot consider a large number of proposals in a given time period; and, when they do vote, their vote covers a multitude of issues all at once.[13]

These objections might be countered by the argument that the assumptions which are not true of the real world do not have any bearing on Tullock's conclusions any way. However, this is false. In particular, the seriatim assumption is the main pillar of his reasoning. If voters consider the entire road program as a whole every so often, instead of voting on individual roadrepair proposals one at a time, their "collective irrationality" disappears. To prove this, let us propose another model in which political parties exist, motivated by the desire to be elected. Each party formulates an over-all road program which it presents to the voters in competition with the programs presented by other parties. The party getting the most votes is allowed to carry out its proposals. Clearly, no voter will support a program which requires him to pay more in taxes than he receives in benefits if a better alternative is available. Hence, no party will formulate a program which requires a majority to do this. It is true that a majority bloc might form and vote roads only for itself, paid for both by itself and by the minority who got no roads. (Tullock also mentions this possibility but rules it out because of his seriatim assumption.) Thus, a minority might find itself sustaining net losses through government action. But this conclusion is vastly different from Tullock's argument that all citizens (or at least a substantial majority) would be net losers. Since the majority would be net gainers, we could not conclude that the government budget was too large. It is clear that the whole burden of Tullock's argument rests upon the voters considering each road-repair bill as an isolated act, separate from other such bills, rather than considering all repairs at once as part of a unified program. This fact remains true whether acts are passed by a majority or by some fraction larger than a majority. Thus, Tullock's major conclusion results from the seriatim assumption, not the majority assumption.

In the real world the seriatim assumption is not valid. Voters elect representatives who pass upon individual acts in a legislature.

However, each representative knows that he must face his constituents at the end of the election period with the net result of all his individual legislative behavior. If he has supported such a high level of road repairs that all his constituents are paying out more than the benefits they receive, he is sure to be defeated by an opponent who promises to reduce the level of repairs and the over-all tax bill so that they balance each other. Thus, the fact that he knows the voters will consider his performance as a whole forces him to prevent the majority of his constituents from winding up net losers from government action. His survival in office is at stake, and politicians place a high value upon survival in office.

Nevertheless, it could be argued that the legislator is faced with the same problem in the assembly that the farmers are in Tullock's model. In the real world, within the legislature itself the first six assumptions behind Tullock's reasoning are all applicable. Only the exclusiveness assumption does not hold true. If we set it aside for the moment, would not each legislator be driven by individual rationality to creating a program for his constituency containing the same over-all imbalance that plagues the farmers in Tullock's model?

To explore this possibility further, we shall borrow a model from an unpublished study by Tullock which analyzes the behavior of a legislature.[14] Assume that there are 100 districts, each composed exactly like the farm community in Tullock's published model. Each district elects, by majority vote, a representative to this state legislature, which decides what road repairs will be made. The legislature considers road-repair programs for individual districts one at a time, and each program which receives the support of a majority passes. The cost of all programs that are passed is spread evenly over all citizens via equal taxes, regardless of the benefits each receives. At the end of the legislative period the individual legislators return to their districts to stand for election "on their records." The citizens of each district do not vote on anything except approval or disapproval of the legislator who has served them – there are no referendums between general elections. Nor are there any other issues before the legislature except the repair of roads.

If successful voting blocs could be formed under these circum-stances, then a minority of 26 percent of the citizens might exploit all the rest, as Tullock points out in his manuscript. In each district 51 farmers could form a solid electoral bloc and elect a representative who would act in their interest only. Then in the legislature 51 of these representatives could form a parliamentary bloc, which would approve a high level of road repairs for the majority in each of their own districts and no repairs for the minority in these districts or for anyone in the 49 non-bloc districts. Thus, 26 percent of the voters would have very well-repaired roads, and 74 percent would have no repairs at all, though the costs were spread over all of them. This startling exploitation of a majority by a minority appears to be the final result of using majority rule.[15]

However, the voting blocs formed in this way would not be stable. The 49 legislators whose constituents were paying taxes but getting no repairs would face certain defeat in their home districts by electoral opponents who would promise to do better. To avoid this catastrophe, they would band together and offer two of the members of the majority bloc extravagantly large road repairs in return for desertion of the old majority bloc and formation of a new one. These two legislators could not resist such an offer. If they did, they would also face electoral defeat at home by opponents who promised to take up the offer – thus providing much better roads for the voters at little added cost. Hence the old majority block would break up, and a new one would form – but it would be vulnerable to the same type of disintegration. As Tullock argues in the case of the farmers, no group of 51 can dominate all other groups; hence no stable majority blocs can be formed at all. Instead, myriads of individual bargains will occur, and each legislator will make "deals" with 50 others to support their road-repair bills in return for their support of his. But this will result in a series of bills passed by "revolving majorities," and each individual legislator will find himself in the same position as are the farmers in Tullock's model. He will calculate the level of repairs to support on the assumption that 51 repair programs will be passed but, in fact 100 will pass (or, at least, many more than 51), and he will discover that the tax load for his district exceeds the gains the district will receive from road repairs. This irrational outcome will occur in every district. Apparently, Tullock's argument applies to legislative government as well as to government by referendum, and we can expect the government budget to be too large in both cases.

However, appearances are deceiving in political theory, because there is one factor at work in this legislative model that is not at work in the model composed of individual farmers: electoral competition. Any legislator who returns to his constituents with a record featuring more costs than benefits is sure to be defeated by an opponent promising the reverse. Thus, the fact that his district emerges from the legislative process with a net loss is not just a marginal loss of utility to him – it is politically fatal. Although each individual farmer might be prepared to absorb a net loss from road referendums as an inevitable result of the system, individual politicians cannot take the same resigned attitude toward electoral defeat.[16]

Instead, they will struggle desperately against losing their offices in one of two ways. First, they can try to reconstitute majority blocs. However, such blocs are inherently unstable, as we have shown. Therefore, this approach offers no permanent solution. Second, they can pass a law which prohibits discriminatory expenditures. Such a law would state that the same standard of road repair must be administered to all roads, just as the costs of these roads are levied against all citizens. This law would prevent any district from emerging from the legislative process with a net loss from the road program (assuming zero administrative costs and an equal number of roads in all districts). Thus, no legislator would be forced to return to his district saddled with a record of loss to his constituents. True, he also could not hope to exploit the citizens of other districts or minorities in his own district in order to "pay off" the majority which elected him. But, faced with the alternatives of non-discrimination or certain defeat, every legislator would find it in his interest to choose the former.

Thus the legislative model can have one of two outcomes: (1) chronic instability can result, with a constant attempt to create majority blocs, which soon dissolve and are replaced by others equally short-lived; or (2) laws against discriminatory spending can be passed. In neither case are Tullock's generalized conclusions valid.[17]

However, the preceding argument is intuitively unsatisfactory because, in the real world, legislatures do not seem to behave this way. On the contrary, logrolling similar to that described by Tullock appears much more realistic than either of the two logically superior outcomes mentioned above. Are we forced, then, to conclude that Tullock's argument is indeed quite applicable to the real world?

The answer is "No." The disproof of Tullock's contentions must take place on two levels: that of a model world and that of the real world. We have already shown that, in Tullock's own model, collective irrationality is not caused by majority rule but by serial voting on a continuous stream of proposals. When the voters choose among road programs periodically on an all-and-once basis, collective irrationality disappears, regardless of whether majority rule is used. Furthermore, the kind of collective irrationality Tullock describes does not arise even if we extend the model to include a legislature. It is not true that the majority is forced into the position of paying more for government action than they get out of it. Thus, on the level of the model world, Tullock's argument that logrolling causes collective irrationality is false. *Ipso facto*, his argument that majority rule causes such irrationality via logrolling must also be false.

This leaves only two of Tullock's contentions about model worlds still standing. Of these, I accept his argument that logrolling (that is, the trading of votes) is to the advantage of its participants and therefore exists when it is legal. But I do not believe that such vote-trading is caused by use of majority rule. To prove this, let us assume that no measure can pass a legislature unless it receives the support of 90 percent of the members. In this case, if 91 percent of the members are mildly in favor of a bill to deport all Jews to Israel (to use Tullock's example) but the other 9 percent are violently opposed, logrolling will still occur. The minority will still seek to protect their interest on issues about which they feel very strongly by trading votes in support of issues to which they are only mildly opposed. The only situation in which no vote-trading of this type would occur is one in which unanimous consent is required for passage of a bill.[18] In that case every minority can protect itself (assuming it has at least one representative in the legislature) without bargaining to do so. But the cost of such protection in terms of equality or representation is high. If there are 100 legislators, and 99 wish to pass a bill but one opposes it, the weight accorded that one is 99 times as great as the weight given each of the others on that issue.

As already pointed out, such unequal weighting of votes is inevitable in any system which requires more than a simple majority for passage of a bill. Yet every such system would also give rise to logrolling. Thus, logrolling is an inescapable result of the following conditions:

1 Two or more different issues are under consideration by an electorate (which may be a legislature).
2 The electorate is small enough to make individual bargaining and vote-trading practical.
3 Individual bargaining and vote-trading are legal.
4 Differing opinions exist among the voters about the issues under consideration.
5 Varying intensities of opinion exist about these issues.
6 The issues are voted upon separately instead of being considered all at once as a unified program.

Whenever these conditions exist simultaneously, logrolling is almost certain to occur. Thus, logrolling is not caused by majority rule but by the existence of the above conditions under any form of rule whatsoever except one-man dictatorship, in which vote-trading cannot occur because only one man votes. But only under majority rule are the preferences of each voter given equal weight in the act of choice. That is why majority rule has been so often adopted as the fairest way to make decisions when opinions differ.

Having disposed of Tullock's contentions in the model world, let us turn to his statements about the real world. Tullock's model appeared more realistic than the model we developed to refute his arguments because his model led to logrolling – which we see everywhere in the real world, whereas our model led to prevention of discriminatory spending – an outcome opposite to that we see in the real world. However, I believe this is the result of assuming that only one issue (road-repairing) exists. If many issues exist, it is not possible for a legislature to pass a law against discriminatory spending. Because the effect of each particular expenditure upon each individual citizen cannot be measured in the same way that the level of road repairs could be, it is inevitable that some bills will benefit certain persons more than others. In fact, most bills in the real world are specifically designed to benefit minority groups. This outcome is unavoidable in a highly differentiated society, where specialization creates minority groups with objective interests which differ widely from each other. Since each minority group seeks to pass certain measures that benefit it specifically, its members agree to trade votes with other minority groups seeking majority support for measures beneficial to them, and logrolling arises. Because logrolling thus occurs in the model we used to refute Tullock when we allow many issues to exist, this model no longer appears less realistic than Tullock's model.

However, the question then becomes whether this process leads to the kind of collective irrationality which Tullock envisages. My answer is that the outcome depends upon whether issues are considered only serially or whether at some point in the process the ultimate electorate makes an all-at-once choice between alternate *over-all* programs of action. In the real world the latter situation prevails; hence, I do not believe that logrolling causes the kind of collective irrationality which Tullock describes.

True, it might do so if certain kinds of ignorance prevail. If, for example, as Tullock mentions in his article, voters are ignorant of some of the costs imposed upon them through indirect taxation, they may vote for a program which includes a government budget that is "really" too large. This would occur because their act of balancing losses to government and gains from it at the margin would be in error, since they would not be taking into account those losses of which they were ignorant. But, if we admit ignorance into the picture, voters may also be ignorant of benefits they receive. As I argue elsewhere, the total effect of ignorance in the real world is, in my opinion, a government budget that is too small.[19]

To sum up our analysis of Tullock's implications about the real-world meaning of his model, we may state the following:

1 Logrolling does exist in the real world, but it is just as compatible with our model as with Tullock's.
2 Logrolling is not caused specifically by simple majority rule but by any type of collective decision-making other than one-man dictatorship.
3 If collective irrationality like that described by Tullock occurs

in the real world, it is not for the reasons Tullock states, because issues are not considered serially by the ultimate electorate in the real world.

4   If such collective irrationality exists in the real world, it is caused by ignorance, and it may take the form of a government budget that is too small as well as one that is too large.

Thus, majority rule is not really the villain Tullock made it out to be. The problems he described as caused by majority rule either do not really exist, are caused by ignorance, or are inherent in the process of collective decision-making, no matter what rule is employed. But only the majority principle guarantees that every vote will have the same weight as every other vote.

III   Reply to a Traditionalist

Anthony Downs's objections to my article and monograph[20] can be divided into three general categories: technical objections to my models, a very strong statement of the traditional argument for majority voting, and the claim that I deduce from my model the conclusion that the government budget as a whole will be too large. I will deal with these objections in order.

Downs begins his attack on my models by restating one of them in the form of seven assumptions. Although I could quarrel with details, I can accept the descriptions for the purposes of the present discussion. Downs's objection to this simple model amounts to pointing out that direct democracy is rather rare in the present-day world.[21] Normally, we elect representatives who meet in some kind of assembly to make political decisions. Downs quite correctly points out that the method of electing representatives violates the seriatim assumption and, consequently, that their election does not fit the model presented in my article. He then turns to the question of whether the model would fit the legislature so elected. He points out that the first six of the assumptions which he has listed as characterizing my model fit a legislature, but he raises questions about the seventh. This assumption is, as Downs points out, relaxed before I reach my general conclusions, and legislatures meet it in its relaxed form. It would thus appear that the model presented in "Problems of Majority Voting" fits the activities of legislatures.

If I properly understand Downs's argument on this point, he agrees that this would be so if it were not for certain aspects of the election process by which the members of the legislature are chosen. In order to discuss this, he turns to one of the models which I introduced in *A Preliminary Investigation of the Theory of Constitutions* (pp. 36–41).[22] He does not explain why he chose that particular one, which would seem rather inappropriate for his purposes. The model assumes there is no "national" party organization capable of exercising disciplinary control over the representatives in the type of legislation normally called "pork barrel."[23] Since Downs wishes to discuss monolithic political parties, another model would have been more convenient.

It must be emphasized that in the model which Downs has chosen to discuss only the majority of the voters in each district are getting their roads repaired, while all the voters pay taxes. It is by no means certain that the majority of the voters in each district are disadvantaged by the system. They might well be better off than they would be under a "strictly fair" distribution of road-repairing. Downs does not discuss this point at all, so I cannot understand his certainty that they would be worse off.

Having presented the model, Downs begins his attack upon it by stating that each district would receive "more costs than benefits" and, consequently, that each legislator would be "sure to be defeated by an opponent promising the reverse." If we grant that the *majority* of the voters were, in fact, worse off, this would still only be true if the electors believed the promises of the opponent. This would require a certain minimum degree of plausibility in those promises. Downs offers two possible sets of promises which the legislators could make and then points out that the first is impossible, thus confining discussion to the second "they can pass a law which prohibits discriminatory expenditures." This was, of course, the first possible remedy to the problem discussed in my article.[24] Downs is rather more enthusiastic about the possibilities here than I am, but the difference concerns only the technical possibilities of defining a "standard of road-repairing." Ignoring such engineering details, our positions are identical. Downs, however, at this point, denies my "generalized conclusions."

"Generalized conclusions" must refer, not to my discussion of uniform standards of road-repairing in the first paragraph on p. 16, but to the second paragraph, which begins, "In the more general and realistic case. . . .' It is my position that the remedy of passing a general law setting a "standard of road-repairing" is possible only if we have a model confined to that single issue. Downs agrees, and he also agrees that in the real world voting is not so confined and, consequently, that the type of logrolling I have described takes place. Thus, Downs and I are, in spite of his verbiage, in complete agreement in analysis of the model.

Having come so far, however, Downs asks "whether this process leads to the kind of collective irrationality which Tullock envisages." His reply is that "the outcome depends upon whether issues are considered only serially or whether at some point in the process the ultimate electorate makes an all-at-once choice between *over-all* programs of action." This sentence is rather confusing. In the model Downs has chosen there is no single "ultimate electorate" but, rather, a series of "ultimate electorates" in each constituency. These select representatives to the legislature on a periodic basis, but these elections are based on past and likely future performance of the candidates as representatives of their districts in the legislature. If by "over-all" Downs means a judgment on *all* the measures passed or likely to be passed in the future, then this does not occur in the model under discussion. The voters choose, not between national parties with national programs, but between local candidates who will represent them in a legislature in which measures are considered seriatim.

There are, of course, political systems in which the voters essentially choose between national parties on the basis of national "platforms." The English system works this way, and, for a number of issues, so does the American. The model which Downs has selected is, in my opinion, the one which fits most closely the situation in the United States with regard to the type of issue which is passed through the legislature by logrolling, but it does not pretend to present the whole of political reality. The situation in which the voters make periodic choices among over-all programs requires a different model.

Democratic political institutions are extremely various and require an almost equally various "vocabulary" of models for their analysis.[25] Downs is perfectly correct in his view that the particular model he has chosen from my monograph does not fit all real-world political situations. Nevertheless, I cannot feel that this is a very serious criticism. Downs's own *An Economic Theory of Democracy* is mainly concerned with a model which is a radically simplified version of the British constitution. It fits the American legislative system very badly indeed, yet this does not prevent me from feeling that it is a major achievement and that it greatly raised our knowledge of "politics."

I should like to end this discussion of the technical differences between Downs and myself by repeating my plea for further research in the field. The models presented so far certainly are only a beginning. Their expansion may well very greatly improve our understanding of the process by which we govern ourselves. This additional research might, possibly, prove that the initial work we have done is in error, but even this would be progress of a sort.

In addition to his criticism of my model, Downs presents with great force the traditional argument for majority voting. He does not present the long and involved chain of reasoning which led me to propose modifications in this rule, nor does he tell the reader what these modifications are. Although I cannot repair the omission in the limited space of this reply, I would like to make two points. In the first place, it is possible to point out defects in a given system even if that system is the best available. Thus, Downs, in his recent "Why the Government Budget is Too Small in a Democracy,"[26] presents what he regards as a systematic defect in democracies without offering any alternative. My analysis of what happens in the present-day world is not affected by my recommendations for possible changes. I could be quite right on the first while totally wrong on the second. Since only my view of the functioning of majority voting is discussed in the original article or that part of my monograph summarized by Downs, my views of what should be done are, strictly speaking, irrelevant. As a matter of fact, at the time I wrote the article, I had no idea of suggesting any changes in voting rules; the recommendation for further research at the end of the article was my single constructive idea.

Downs's vigorous defense of simple majority voting may have had its origin in an unfortunate sentence near the end of my article. The sentence, in which I say that "the problem . . . arises from . . . compelling the minority to accept the will of the majority," is wrong, and I apologize for it. It is not correct to say that the outcome of a chain of reasoning arises from any single one of the premises. By the same token, Downs's efforts to prove that the real cause lies in the seriatim assumption fail. Both assumptions are necessary for the particular model presented in "Problems of Majority Voting." Other models in which either or both assumptions are omitted are also of use for research in this area.

A more serious criticism of Downs's presentation of the traditional view of majority voting, however, concerns a series of paradoxes within the process of majority voting itself.[27] The majority rule appears to be simple, but careful analysis has uncovered a series of serious mathematical difficulties which make the traditional view which Downs presents untenable. It may be that the problems posed by Arrow and Black will eventually be solved,[28] but, until they are, arguments for simple majority voting rest on a perilous foundation.

My final point concerns Downs's belief that my model leads to the conclusion that the governmental budget as a whole will be too large. In the special case of road-repairing this is correct, but in the more general case it is not. My discussion of fiscal problems under a generalized model (pp. 17–18) indicates that some parts of the budget would be irrationally large and others irrationally small. Neither in the article nor in the monograph do I offer the opinion that the budget as a whole is too large.

2

An Economic Analysis of Political Choice

It is sometimes hard to follow extremely abstract reasoning in a new field. Since the field to be discussed is new to most economists[1] I have decided to begin by discussing a concrete example rather than presenting an abstract and fully general model. Constitutional problems of a small and rather peculiar community will be discussed in the early part of the article. The theory developed of this particular community will then be converted into a general model.

Consider, then, a community of 100 farmers owning more or less equivalent farms who live in a township cut by a number of main highways. These highways are maintained by the state government, but they are limited-access roads and can be entered only from local road. These local roads are the responsibility of the township. Four or five farmers are dependent on each of the local roads to reach the main highways. The maintenance and improvement of these roads is the only political problem of the township and, as our final restriction, the taxing power of the township government is limited to a general property tax which will mean that costs will be relatively equally shared by all the farmers.[2] The question to be discussed is: what would be the ideal voting rule for these farmers to use in determining which roads will be repaired or improved?

One possible rule, which has simplicity if nothing else to commend it, would be to let any individual order repairs or improvements on any road he wished. Thus, any farmer could simply call up the township government and order some road-repair project and the cost would then be assessed to all the farmers. Since each farmer would be able to get his own road repaired while paying only 1 percent of the cost under this rule, I presume it is obvious to an audience of economists that there would be vast overinvestment in road facilities. We would have a Galbraithian world in which splendid highways connected hovels and in which the congestion problem had been solved by putting cars with tail fins beyond the purse of most farmers. The costs of this overinvestment on the farmers we will call "external costs" and we will find that there is an external cost for every voting rule short of unanimity.

A method of improving the situation would be to require that several farmers agree on each road maintenance project. This would mean, of course, that some time would be spent in negotiating the agreement, but let us for the time being ignore the problems of reaching agreement and concentrate our attention on the results that could be expected if the parties were able to reach agreements costlessly. Increasing the number of farmers required to agree to a given repair or maintenance job would make only a minor difference as long as the number was small enough so that those farmers living on a given road are sufficient to get it repaired. Let us, therefore, consider a rule requiring ten farmers to agree to any given road-repairing project, which would insure that farmers along at least two roads would have to agree.

Clearly, the farmers along one road could get agreement to its repairs from the farmers on another only by promising to agree to the repair of the other road. If this is so, then they must count the cost of repairing the other road as part of the cost of repairing their own. Thus, the real cost to them of repairing their road is something close to 10 percent of the total cost. (An easy way of thinking of this process is to consider how much the voter, under various rules, must pay in taxes for each $100.00 worth of road repairing. Under the one-voter choice rule he would have to pay $1.00, under our present ten-voter rule $10.00 and under a unanimity rule, $100.00.)

Clearly, with our new ten-voter rule, the amount of road repairing undertaken would be much less than with the single-voter rule, and, hence, the external cost imposed on each member of the community would be less. (It may appear peculiar to refer to this cost as "external" since in normal usage the term usually refers to some private activity, not to governmental action, but a little reflection will indicate that government action can impose external costs. If I am taxed to pay farmers subsidies so that they will reduce their production and thus raise my food costs, clearly I am suffering an external cost under the usual definitions of the term. The really peculiar phenomenon is the failure of economists in the past to use external costs in discussing political decisions, not our present usage.)[3]

Our community, of course, can require more than ten voters to agree to any given road repair or improvement project. Each increase in the number required to agree will increase the number of necessary parties to a bargain, and hence raise the cost to each individual of a given amount of road repairing. The larger the number of farmers required to agree, the closer the cost of having his road repaired to each individual farmer will approach the real cost. Hence, the less wastage of resources and the less external cost imposed on the farmers. We can represent this process by an idealized curve with the external cost of the voting rule very high at the single-voter extreme and zero at the unanimity end (see figure 2.1).

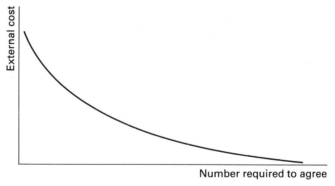

Figure 2.1

Note that the curve in figure 2.1 is perfectly smooth; there is no kink or irregularity at the mid-point. In view of the role played by simple majority voting in most of our present political ideology, this is most interesting. I would devote more attention to the simple majority case which is given so much emphasis by traditional political scientists if I had not already published an article, "Problems of Majority Voting" in the *Journal of Political Economy*,[4] giving an analysis of that particular point on the curve. Perhaps it would be better to say that the present paper is consistent with "Problems of Majority Voting" rather than the other way around since it was my discovery that simple majority voting led to external costs which started me on the chain of reasoning which we are now reviewing.

Note that in figure 2.1 there are external costs for every voting rule except unanimity. Only by requiring unanimous agreement for each road-repair project could we make certain that the cost to the "decision-makers" and the real cost coincided, and hence eliminate overinvestment. In the real world, of course, requring unanimity would be impractical because of the problem of obtaining unanimous agreement. This brings us to the problem of the investment of resources in bargaining. Again, we are in an area which has been largely overlooked by economists. Clearly, chaffering and higgling consume resources; equally clearly, in choosing between two possible social arrangements the amount of this type of cost to be expected under each is a relevant consideration. Nevertheless, the subject has been almost completely overlooked in economic discussions, probably because these costs in economic matters are frequently insignificant in magnitude. There has been some discussion of whether bargaining problems might not be so severe in certain cases as to make reaching of agreement impossible, but that is all.[5]

Regardless of the reasons which have led to this subject being almost ignored by economists, it is highly important for our present investigation and consequently must be discussed at some length. One cost of bargaining which may sometimes be overlooked is the loss of desirable opportunities due to a failure to conclude the deal. Clearly, any decision rule will sometimes lead to desirable proposals failing and presumably the number of such proposals which would fail would be a positive function of the difficulty of reaching agreement under a series of different rules. Turning to more obvious costs, the actual process of bargaining and reaching agreement certainly consumes resources, and this again would be a positive function of the difficulty of reaching agreement.

Let us now reconsider possible decision rules for our small

community of farmers from the bargaining cost aspect. Our simplest rule, permitting any individual to order road repairs, would involve no bargaining costs. If agreement of two persons were required, this would surely impose some bargaining costs and these costs would increase as the number of people required to agree was raised. It should be remembered that bargaining costs have been defined to include the "cost" resulting from a failure to make bargains which, in the abstract, would be desirable. Thus, we can draw a cost of bargaining curve similar to our external cost curve (see figure 2.2). It, of course, has the opposite slant from the external cost curve.

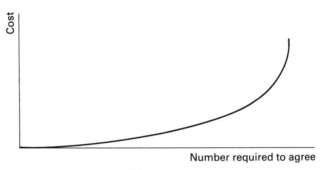

Figure 2.2

The rather odd shape of this curve, as I have drawn it, requires some explanation. The basic reason is simply that the bargaining situation at unanimity or near-unanimity is radically different from that where the number required to agree is smaller. To take the extreme case, if the agreement of only two farmers is required for a road-repair project, there is apt to be little bargaining in the normal meaning of the term. Each party will be fully aware that the other can readily turn to someone else if his terms are too high. In consequence, the process of higgling in this case is likely to involve little actual bargaining, in the sense of trying to beat prices down (or up). The simple procedure if the first person you approach asks too much for his support is to go to someone else. As long as there are plenty of possible alternatives, there is no reason to waste time trying to bargain with some individual. Thus, in the lower range, the investment of resources in bargaining is likely to take the form, predominantly, of time and effort spent in trying to get the best terms by obtaining information on possible alternatives. Obviously, investment in higgling and chaffering would increase exponentially as the number required to agree increase in this range, but at a relatively moderate rate.

To turn to the other extreme, unanimity, this means that each farmer is an essential party to the agreement. Since each farmer has a monopoly of an essential resource, his consent, each farmer can aim at obtaining the entire benefit of the agreement for himself. Bargaining, in the sense of trying to maneuver people into accepting lower returns than they would desire by argument, is the only resource which the farmers can use under these circumstances, and it seems highly likely that agreement would normally be impossible. Certainly, the direct costs of making such an agreement would be extremely high and, if we count the likelihood that no agreement will be reached and hence that no roads will be repaired, the bargaining costs would probably approach infinity. This, of course, is the extreme, but somewhat similar conditions would begin to develop as the number of parties required to approve road repair projects approached 100. As a result, we have a cost line with the rather peculiar shape I have drawn.

With these two cost functions, we can obtain a general cost curve for any voting rule on our continuum by simple geometric addition (see figure 2.3). The low point on this curve would indicate for each individual voter, as well as for "society in general," if that phrase has any definite meaning, the optimum

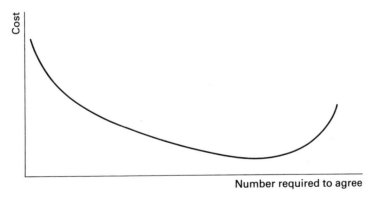

Figure 2.3

rule. At that point, the costs of the political process, including the opportunity costs of lost chances for carrying out beneficial projects, would be minimized.

Economists in discussing resource allocation by government have traditionally recommended the matching of marginal cost and benefit without, however, considering the political process which would lead to such a decision.[6] We have approached the problem from the other direction beginning with the political process, nevertheless, we end up with what is really an improved version of the traditional marginal criteria. Our minimum point differs from the traditional matching of marginal costs and benefits in only two respects: we specify whose value jugments are to be used in measuring cost and benefit and we include additional costs arising out of the political process of decision-making. From the standpoint of any individual, decisions made under our 'ideal' decision-making rule will result in the marginal cost to him of road repairing equalling the marginal benefit he receives.[7] The inclusion of intrinsic political costs imposed by the decision-making process itself among the total costs to be considered seems reasonable and our procedure guarantees that this "non-traditional" cost will be minimized.

Now we have completed our survey of our peculiar small community's political problems and produced a theory which would permit its citizens to select their ideal "constitution." Let us see if we cannot extend our reasoning to a more general and realistic model. In the first place, it is clear that our model is not bound solely to road repairing. Any project which uses general revenues to benefit a minority of the people would lead to the same results. Since such projects make up the overwhelming majority of modern legislation, this means that our model is of considerable practical value. Further consideration, however, leads to the conclusion that the model has an even wider application, it is not limited to fiscal measures, but also applies to all cases where minorities favor various measures and where the intensity of their desire for these measures is such that they would engage in vote-trading to get them enacted. This still further widens the scope of our model.

Thus, the theory covers all cases where there is a minority whose desires are more intense than those of the majority. Surely, this covers the overwhelming majority of all the legislative activity of Congress, but equally surely it does not cover all. Situations in which intensity of desires were more or less equally distributed must occur, even if they are rare. They are susceptible to analysis using much the same tools we have utilized in the intense minority case. I cannot present this analysis here because of shortage of time, but I can say that the results are different from but not inconsistent with those we have been discussing. The same may be said for the extremely rare case in which the majority feels more strongly than the minority.

Thus, it would appear that we have a good theoretical system for simple direct democracy governments. Such simple governments do, of course, exist. The New England town meeting is one example and the village assemblies which are so common in Asia provide another. Nevertheless, most major democracies use representative rather than direct democracy, and the question arises whether they also can be analyzed by the same methods. The answer to the question is, fortunately, yes. Using the same principles as those used in this paper, it is possible to develop complex models which involve representative democracy, parties, two-house legislatures, and federal-state division of authority. These complex models, which cannot be presented in a single article, permit analysis of existing constitutions and their comparison with other existing or proposed organizational structures.[8] The field is, to me, a highly exciting one because it seems likely that further research will lead to the discovery of methods of improving the efficiency of democratic governments. Since such improvements would be of great benefit to each of us, it seems that research in this new field should be encouraged.

3

Entry Barriers in Politics

The question, "What is the difference between a political party and a department store?" sounds like a riddle, but I suggest it as a serious subject for inquiry. The two types of organization clearly are very different, and specifying the differences is a good exercise for an economist who is interested in applying the tools of his trade to the study of politics. The subject of this paper came to me while I was engaged in just this exercise (which may or may not be regarded as a recommendation). One of the conspicuous differences is that the department store will normally own its own plant, while the political party does not. The political party may, of course, own some office furniture, but this is only a tiny part of the capital that it will use to serve its customers if it is successful in the competitive struggle. This difference between the political party and the department store is such an obvious one that, like the purloined letter, it is almost invisible. We are also so accustomed to it, that a question as to why it should exist may seem eccentric, but, as I hope to demonstrate, it has an economically interesting answer. This is one field where an essentially political problem can be treated entirely as an economic problem, specifically as an example of the problem of controlling natural monopolies. Looked at in this way, we will see that there is a method of controlling natural monopolies which has not been much discussed by economists but which has been in use by practical men for many years.

Three techniques are normally suggested for dealing with natural monopolies: we can leave them alone, letting their mangers do as they wish, we can subject them to regulation, or they can be publicly owned and operated. If you will bear with me in considering the government itself as a natural monopoly, it will be obvious that none of these techniques are suitable for dealing with it. Leaving the monopoly alone, which if we are talking about government means a despotic state, is not at all impossible. In fact, this has been by far the commonest way of handling the problem if we consider the whole of man's history. I suspect, however, that there is no one, no matter how devoted to laissez faire, who will advocate this solution for this type of natural monopoly. In a sense the whole point of democracy is to prevent this sort of "free enterprise."

If the extreme libertarians will not favor free enterprise, it is also an area where devotees of *dirigisme* will not favor controls. It is, of course, a little hard to see who would do the controlling in this case, and who would control the (presumed) monopoly of controlling would be even harder, but I doubt that any democrat, no matter how devoted to planning and controls, would favor controls even if these technical problems could be solved. This is one area where we all favor unrestrained consumer sovereignty. The preoccupation which economists have had since Bentham with improving the information of the parties to a transaction would not be out of place in this area. Efforts to prevent direct fraud would also seem to be sensible, although experience seems to indicate that little can be done on these lines. But these are the same sorts of thing which we hope for in purely competitive industries, not measures to control a monopoly. The third alternative – public ownership and operation – raises difficult problems of definition. It is not at all clear what a proposal to subject a successful political party to public ownership and operation would mean. The government surely is publicly owned already, and whether it is publicly operated depends upon the definition of public in this particular usage. I am inclined to think that our present set of institutions could best be described as public ownership with private operation.

One of the handy definitions of government is "the monopoly of force." Those of us who have been engaged in what we call synergetics – or the present invasion of political theory by economists – have begun to wonder whether the force really must be monopolized. There seem to be a surprising number of private policemen in New York, and a good deal of our national defense establishment is handled by private companies under contract. It may be that some governmental activities are not so necessarily monopolistic as has been generally thought. Leaving this problem aside, however, clearly a good many of the activities undertaken by governments are natural monopolies. Further, under democratic procedures, the elected members of the government always exercise a sort of monopoly due to the simple fact that there is only one set of them elected. Judge Smith has a monopoly of representing the city of Charlottesville, Virginia, in the House of Representatives. A small group of rather estimable gentlemen have a monopoly of governing the city of Charlottesville, and Mr Johnson has a monopoly of a whole set of governmental activities. The situation is, perhaps, clearer in a parliamentary government where a single party or coalition has complete control over all governmental activities. The natural monopoly here comes from a technological consideration which amounts to a very strong economy of scale: only one majority can exist at a time.

Let us now consider this problem simply as one in economics.[1] Suppose we have an industry, say cement manufacturing, in a small, isolated country in which economies of scale are strong enough so that a company having more than half of the market could operate on a lower cost level than any smaller competitor. Further, to make our analogy complete, assume that the cost advantage would continue up to full market control by one company. If the industry is a vital one where we fear the results of simply leaving it alone, if regulation is ruled out, and if public control is impossible, what can we do?

The problem, of course, is simply an extreme entry barrier. Presumably a competitor could come in and drive the present occupant of the market into bankruptcy by violent competition, but it would be an expensive and risky thing to do. The competitor would have to build a new plant and invest a good deal of funds in the staying alive through the cut-throat competition phase, and he would have no assurance of winning out, let alone making enough from the ensuing monopoly to pay him back for his expenditure. Clearly the company in occupation of the natural monopoly would not be completely free from restraints, but equally clearly only really monumental inefficiency would really much endanger its position.[2]

Looked at from the standpoint of the public of the small island country, this situation would clearly be unsatisfactory, but we have barred them from the traditional remedies. There remains an alternative. They could build or buy a cement plant and periodically put its operation up to auction. In its simplest form this auction could require as a bid simply the price which the entrepreneurial company would charge for cement during the coming year. The lowest bidder would get the right to operate the plant. This, of course, would leave open to the operator letting the plant run down through undermaintenance. We might deal with this problem by having the small country specify the amount and type of maintenance which would have to be undertaken during the year before the bidding. This, however, would involve partial management of the plant by the country, and in any event it is not much like what goes on in the political sphere. Another procedure would be to have the bid include not only the price at which the cement was to be sold but also statements about maintenance, introduction of improvements, etc. The entrepreneurial group who would be permitted to operate the plant would be selected on the basis of a judgment as to which of these rather involved bids was, in all-round terms, the best. Naturally this complicated type of "bidding" raises difficult problems of judgment, but in the governmental case it is hard to see any alternative which is superior. This is, in fact, the type of complex judgment which we normally make in market transactions. In buying a car I cannot simply choose the cheapest; I must balance one package of attributes, including price, against another. The choice of the best "bidder" would be similar. The principle difference would be the unenforceable nature of the promises made by the political "entrepreneurs."

Putting the whole transaction in strictly economic terms, we have an industry with an extremely high entry barrier. Public provision of the capital plant artificially reduces that barrier. With the new lower barrier, competition and potential competition will enter much more strongly into the calculations of the present management than it would without this reduction. The small island community could depend upon the cost of its cement being considerably lower than under laissez faire. The problems that would arise would be, essentially, problems of consumer judgment for a complex product and problems of aggregating preferences. The situation would be one of monopoly only insofar as there was a remaining entry barrier even when the plant was provided. Ignoring the latter class of problems for the moment, decisions as to which of the "bids" was best would be similar to ordinary consumer choice in principle, but more complex in practice. A genuine technical judgment on the desirability of the replacement of some given machine in this period or the next would be necessary in some cases. Whether replacement of present equipment by new would be worthwhile would unfortunately be a decision that the "consumer" would have to make. Further, these decisions have to be made prospectively, not retrospectively. If I am considering buying a Chrysler with a turbine engine, I can at least look at and try an existing car just like the one I would buy. This would not be so with our cement plant if new equipment were proposed. Thus we could and should anticipate less successful judgment of the bids than we find in more normal market situations. This is, of course, realistic. It is true that most people's judgment on whether the Republicans or the Democrats will serve them best is less accurate than their judgment on the same question about a car they are thinking of buying.

The problems of aggregating preferences simply complicate the situation further. They make the judgment of the consumers even less skillful. The fact that this judgment is a relatively poor one raises some special problems. It is sensible for the entrepreneurs who are bidding for the use of the plant to take the relatively uninformed state of the people who will judge the bids into account. Deception and distortion will be easier under these circumstances than in the marketplace. As one example, let us consider the so-called "going concern" value of the plant. If a new group takes over the plant, it will normally be more efficient for them to retain most of the labor force and lower management rather than hire and train new personnel. If the bids were submitted to highly qualified personnel for judgment, no doubt they would be able to require performance which could only be reached by highly efficient operations, and hence the workers and lower management would be taken over by the new group of entrepreneurs. If, however, the people making the judgment as to which bid was best were not highly qualified – and the voters certainly are not – then various rather inefficient provisions might be inserted into the bid. The successful entrepreneurs might, for example, specify that they would work for a fixed fee instead of for a residual.

This procedure might seem silly, but it is a fact that most elected officials do work for fixed fees. This may be simply due to the difficulty of computing anything comparable to a profit on the government's operations, but it may also be because the voters somehow feel that this is a better system. In many types of government contract where profit as a residual would seem the obvious choice a fixed fee or contract renegotiation has in fact been adopted, apparently to please the voters. But regardless of the reasons for it, this fixed fee system together with a system of judging bids which is not highly skilled gives the political entrepreneur a motive for behavior which, on the surface, would appear to be simply inefficient. Putting people on the payroll not in terms of their contribution to the enterprise but in terms of their contribution to the entrepreneur would be a quite sensible way of capturing profits not available under the fixed fee system.

The obvious answer to this problem is simply improving the standards by which the bids are judged. If the various entrepreneurs must submit their bids to the scrutiny of real experts (although whether experts are actually ever this good is questionable), they would have to plan on the most efficient methods of management in order to beat out their competitors. Ruling this method out as impractical in a democracy,[3] the only two expedients that seem to remain are simply to let the entrepreneurs do this if it pays them or give the workers and lower management some sort of civil service status. Both expedients have severe drawbacks. Since the disadvantages of a civil service system are, for some reason, normally not discussed, a few words on them might be helpful. The higher management, being unable to discharge the workers without some sort of elaborate procedure, will be less effective. If the civil service system amounts to permanent tenure, as it does in the United States, then the real control that the higher management has over the lower is apt to be much less than optimum. It may, of course, still be better than simply ignoring the problem. The purchase of goods for government use raises somewhat the same problem, although simply requiring bidding may provide a suitable solution.

But to return to the subject of entry barriers and the economics of monopoly, the company now operating the cement plant would have one advantage over any group of entrepreneurs contemplating bidding against them for the next period. They already have a management in existence which has some "going concern" value of its own. The potential competitors will have to establish such an organization simply for the purpose of making their bid. Thus the potential competitor will need to invest some resources into preparing for the competition which will not be required of the present operators. Although the entry barrier has been lowered by the public ownership of the plant, it has not been reduced to zero. This means that the existing management – and the competitors, for that matter – can afford to put their bid somewhat above the "pure competition" level because of this impediment to competition. Indeed, if the profits from managing the enterprise are small, which would be so either if the bid system worked very well or if payment was by a relatively small fixed fee and side-payments were prohibited, then even a very low entry barrier might be sufficient to keep the effective level of potential competition low. In most modern democracies the legally available rewards of office are fairly low, considering the size of the enterprise. This prevents large monopoly profits but also eliminates the normal incentives for efficiency. Under these circumstances competition is needed, not to prevent exploitation, but to keep the management on its toes. Thus we might find these entry barriers still too high and look for an expedient to lower them still further.

Perhaps, however, it might be wise to remind ourselves of the exact problem we are examining. Many governmental services are natural monopolies, and economists are naturally apt to think of them when we discuss problems in this general area. Our monopoly, however, is the government itself, not its constituent services. It is a monopoly simply because we can have only one cabinet, governor, mayor, president, or majority in a legislature. The scale advantage which acts as a barrier to entry is the majority voting rule[4] which provides that the "entrepreneurial group" which obtains half the customers can drive the other entrepreneurial group or groups out of the market. This is the basic reason we must depend upon potential competition rather than upon real competition. This is also the reason why there may well be only two competitors – the present occupant and a potential replacement – instead of many competing "firms." The problem of public policy we are discussing in this essay is insuring that the entry barrier is low enough so that this potential competition is a real restriction on the activities of the present occupant of the monopoly.

The problem is that there may not be any significant potential competition. This fact is not very obvious because we normally think of national politics, and during our lifetime there has always been an active opposition party.[5] If we turn to local politics, however, we will frequently observe a complete absence of organized opposition. Charlottesville, for example, has normally only one serious set of candidates for the city council. The job of city councilman, of course, is unsalaried; so the only attractions are the nonpecuniary rewards of office. I suspect that the pecuniary and nonpecuniary pains of running for office and being beaten are, in net, much greater than the non-pecuniary gains of being a councilman. It is also quite hard for a potential opposition individual or slate to even get his name and platform before the voters, let alone persuading them that it is sensible to vote for him or them.[6] Under the circumstances it is not surprising that there are few opposition candidates.

The obvious way of insuring potential competition in an organized form would be to raise the rewards of office to a level where they would be worth more than the organizational costs of an opposition group properly discounted by the risks involved. This might be quite expensive, and democracies have characteristically not followed this course of action. Compensation for electoral success – legal compensation, anyway – has normally been quite modest. Another technique would be to pay a potential opposition group. In the very direct form of the official salary for the leader of the opposition in Britain, this procedure has been rare, but in a more indirect way it is the common system. If quite a number of offices are put up for vote, it is fairly certain, human nature being what it is, that one organized group will not get all of them. The

occupants of the other offices will receive compensation[7] and will also be in positions where they can fairly easily make their counter proposals to the government's policies known to the voters. Their actual existence and the practice of public debates in legislative bodies makes it unlikely that the present occupants of the monopoly will behave as though they had a highly secure position. Whether this is a cheaper way of getting a given quality of entrepreneurial ability than offering higher rewards to those in power I cannot say, but it certainly works.

Looked at from this standpoint, the purpose of providing offices for the opposition is to effectively lower the entry barrier by paying part of the organization costs of the potential entrant. Parliamentary debates have the function of simply keeping the existence of a well-organized potential competitor continually before the mind of the government and of providing publicity for the offers of the opposition and government for the next decision period. The system is neat in that no device need be introduced to select the potential competitors who will be supported as opposed to those who will not. The elections select both the government and the opposition. People who do not get elected at all are not supported. Further, the opposition is not motivated to simply settle down to professional opposition because the rewards of office are greater than those of opposition while the costs of trying to replace the present occupants of the monopoly are not significantly greater than the costs of simply holding on.

It is possible to argue that this sytem would be more efficient if there were more than two competitors. The European systems with many parties give the government to a coalition of parties, and each present member of the coalition competes with each party out of office because it is always possible to make up a new coalition. Whether this really leads to more effective competition, given the fact that the coalitions themselves are the governments while the voters vote for the parties, is not at all certain. In any event, the various systems all do provide for public support for the organizational costs of a potential competitor and hence keep the entry barrier low. Here is one place where potential competition is obviously highly effective, but only because of intelligent public policy.

This paper has, in a sense, been an exercise in applying

economic analysis to a completely noneconomic area. In our universities as they are now organized the subject matter of my paper, political organization, is taught in one department and the techniques of analysis I have employed are taught in another. It is probably for this reason that the rather simple and straightforward line of reasoning I have presented has never before been brought out. In this area, as in so many others, practical men have solved problems that the theorists have not even thought of. It seems to me that this paper is a simple but plain demonstration of the need for some change in our present ways of organizing knowledge. Economists who are interested in politics and political theorists who have a command of economic tools can perform research which is impossible for the more traditionally trained man. I am, in a sense, preaching to the converted, but I am asking you to go out and preach the gospel to all the nations.

Discussion

In the published discussion of this panel it is notable that Professor Robert L. Bishop and Professor Jesse Markham devoted almost all of their attention to John Harsanyi's piece on game theory. Bishop's only response to my paper is a single sentence in his discussion of Harsanyi, "it is interesting to note, Professor Tullock's rather casually expressed opinion to the contrary: 'only one majority can exist at a time.'" He said nothing about Anthony Down's paper.

Jesse W. Markham had one paragraph about the Tullock paper as follows.

> Tullock's main point that the economic concept of barriers to entry can profitably be applied to political situations could, I believe, have profited from the use of some of Harsanyi's analytical tools. His point is that in holding down entry barriers confronting other parties we (the public) secure for ourselves responsible government by the "monopolists" (party in power) through the beneficial pressures of potential competition. Since democratic systems provide for public support of political parties, we have an intelligent public policy that keeps entry barriers low. But does this necessarily follow in cases of two (or more) party systems where

barriers may be relative rather than absolute? If voters (or, more correctly, contributors to political parties) reason that contributions to the "in" party yield a bigger payoff (a higher expected utility) than if made to the "out" or "potential" party, the "war chests" of the "in" party may become insuperable barriers whereas a public policy levying a special tax on party contributions may simply make entry difficult but relatively easier.

There was then a very short paragraph about Downs and he closed with the following general reamrks.

In all societies a choice must be made as to which activities will be assigned to the market for solution and which will be solved by nonmarket criteria. Market solutions are typically imperfect, but when we observe the frightening possible consequences of nonmarket decision-making, we are likely to accept the solutions of reasonably competitive markets with renewed faith, and urge, as it seems to me Tullock does, that they be used more extensively and for a wider range of social problems.

That two such prominent discussants almost totally ignored the two Public Choice papers is evidence of how little impression the subject had made at that time.

4

The General Irrelevance of the General Impossibility Theorem

A phantom has stalked the classrooms and seminars of economics and political science for nearly 15 years. This phantom, Arrow's general impossibility theorem, has been generally interpreted as proving that no sensible method of aggregating preferences exists.[1] The purpose of this essay is to exorcise the phantom, not by disproving the theorem in its strict mathematical form, but by showing that it is insubstantial. I shall show that when a rather simple and probable type of interdependence is assumed among the preference functions of the choosing individuals, the problem becomes trivial if the number of voters is large.[2] Since most cases which require aggregation of preferences involve large numbers of people, "Arrow problems" will seldom be of much importance.

In *Social Choice and Individual Values*[3] Arrow included a chapter on "Similarity as the Basis of Social Welfare Judgments"[4] in which he discussed possible lines of research which might lead to a method of avoiding the implications of his proof. In this chapter, he pointed to Black's single-peaked preference curves as particularly promising.[5] The generalization of Black's single-peaked curves to more than one dimension will give the fundamental model upon which this article is based. It may, therefore, fairly be said that the present work follows the path indicated by Arrow. The development of single-peaked preferences for two dimensions was first undertaken by Newing and Black in *Committee Decisions with Complementary Valuation*,[6] which was published at about the same time as *Social Choice and Individual Values* and presumably was not known to Arrow. Newing and Black, however, did not give much consideration to cases in which there were large numbers of voters. The model to be used here will involve many voters and will be used to examine the general impossibility theorem.

The proof of Arrow's theorem requires, as one of its steps, the cyclical majority or paradox of voting.[7] In addition to the mathematical reasons, the emphasis on the paradox is appropriate since the method of "aggregating preferences" which immediately occurs to the average citizen of a democracy is majority voting. This article is intended to demonstrate that majority voting will, indeed, always be subject to the paradox of voting, but that this is of very little importance. Majority voting will not produce a "perfect" answer, but the answer it does produce will not be significantly "worse" than if the paradox of voting did not exist. Any choice process involving large numbers of people will surely be subject to innumerable minor defects with the result that the outcome, if considered in sufficient detail, will always deviate from Arrow's conditions. The deviation may, however, be so small that it makes no practical difference.

Most majority voting procedures have arrangements which bring the voting to an end before every tiny detail of the proposal has been subject to a vote. These rules (frequently informal rather than part of the rules of order) mean that when the voting is brought to a stop there almost certainly remain minor changes in the result which a majority would approve if it were possible to bring them to a vote. Thus the outcome will be, in Arrow's terms, imposed, but it will be very close to a perfect result. As an example, suppose a body of men is voting on the amount of money to be spent on something, with the range under consideration running from zero to $10,000,000. The preferences of these men are single-peaked. Majority voting will eventually lead to the selection of the optimum of the median voter as the outcome. If, however, the procedure is such that proposals to change the amount of money by $100 or less cannot be entertained,[8] then the outcome will normally not be at the optimum, but it will be within $100 of it. This result does not meet Arrow's conditions, but there is no reason to be disturbed by this fact.

In order to demonstrate that the cyclical majority is equally unimportant in real world "preference aggregation," let us consider a group of voters deciding two matters, say appropriations for the army and the navy by majority voting. In figure 4.1 the vertical dimension is the appropriation for the army and the horizontal for the navy. The individual voters each have an optimum combination and a preference mountain which has the usual characteristics. For simplicity let us further assume that the voter's optima are evenly distributed over the space, and that their indifference curves are all perfect circles centering on their optima. The last two assumptions do not correspond with reality and will be eliminated at a later stage. Let us further assume that the number of voters is great enough so that the space can serve as a proxy for the voters. Putting it differently, of two areas in the issue space of figure 4.1, the larger will contain the optima of more voters than will the smaller. This makes it possible to use simple Euclidean geometry as an analytical tool.

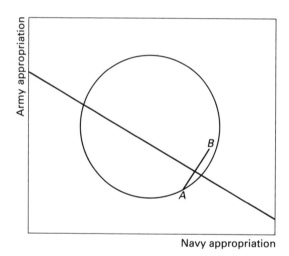

Figure 4.1

Suppose we wish to determine whether motion *B* on figure 4.1 can defeat the status quo, represented by *A*, by a simple majority vote. Since we are assuming that all indifference curves are perfect circles around the individual's optimum, each voter will simply vote for the alternative which is closest to his optimum. If we connect *A* and *B* with a straight line and erect a perpendicular bisector on this line, then *B* will be closer to the optima of all individuals whose optima lie on the same side of the bisector as *B* and *A* will similarly be closest to all optima which lie on *A*'s side of the bisector. We can compare the votes for each alternative by simply noting the area of the rectangle on each side of the bisector. As a shorthand method, if the perpendicular bisector runs through the center of the rectangle there will be an equal number of votes for *A* and *B*. If it does not, then the alternative on the same side of the perpendicular bisector as the center will win. The locus of all points which will tie with *A* is a circle around the center running through *A*, and *A* can beat any point outside the circle but will be beaten by any point inside. Clearly no cycles are possible. The process will lead into the center eventually, since, of any pair of alternatives, the one closer to the center will always win.

This might be called the perfect geometrical model, in which the number of voters whose optima fall in a given area is exactly proportional to its area. Given that the voters are finite in number, small discontinuities would appear. Two areas that differ little in size might have the same number of voters; indeed, the smaller might even have more. Cycles are, therefore, possible, but they would become less and less important as the number of choosing individuals increases. In figure 4.2 we have a point, *A*, in our standard type of issue space, and I have drawn a circle around it. For convenience I shall assume 999,999 voters. Whether any given

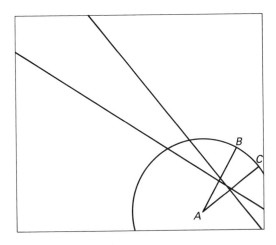

Figure 4.2

point on this circle can beat *A* depends upon how the perpendicular bisector of the line connecting it with *A* partitions the voters' optima. We can conceive ourselves as moving around the circle, trying each point on it against *A*. *B* would beat *A*, but *C* would not. With a finite number of voters, the changes between motions would be discontinuous. *B*, for example, might get 602,371 votes to *A*'s 397,628. As we moved around the circle towards *C* there would be a small space in which this vote would stay unchanged, then it would suddenly shift to 602,370 against 397,629, which would also persist for a short segment of the circle. Needless to say, the segment in which the vote did not change, would be extremely small, but it would exist.

If we consider a point which gets only a bare majority over *A*, 500,000 votes to 499,999, and move along the circle towards *B*, there will be a finite gap during which the vote does not change, and then it will shift to 500,000 for *A* and 499,999 for the alternative.[9] Given this finite distance, however, it is sure that at least occasionally a point can be beaten by another point which is more distant from the center than it is. In other words, it will be possible for majority voting to move away from the center as well as to move towards it. This phenomenon makes cycles possible.[10]

Granting these discontinuities, however, we could still draw a line separating those points which could get a majority over any given point from those that could not. With our 999,999 voters this line would no doubt appear to be the circle of figure 4.1 to the naked eye. Examining it through a microscope, however, we should find that it was not exactly circular and that there would be small areas which could get a majority over the original point, but which lay farther from the center than that point. Note, however, that these areas would be very small. If our original point is far from the center (as in *A* in either figure 4.1 or figure 4.2), then the area which could get a majority over *A* but which lies farther from the center would be tiny compared with the area which could get a majority and which lay closer to the center.

Under these circumstances, unless proposals for changes are introduced in a very carefully controlled and planned manner, the voting process would in all probability lead to rapid movement toward the center.[11] Unfortunately the convergence need not continue until the absolute center is reached.[12] For close to the center, the area which is preferred to A and is closer to the center, is much smaller than initially. It is therefore more probable than at first that the preferred alternative to A would be farther from the center than A. Cycling becomes more probable. When we get very close to the center a point randomly selected from among those which could get a majority over the given point would have a good chance of being farther from the center than it is. At this point, however, most voters will feel that new proposals are splitting hairs, and the motion to adjourn will carry.

Discussion of the point is simplified by the use of a particular type of line which we will call a "median line." A median line is a line passing through two individuals' optima and dividing the remaining optima either into two equal "halves" or, if the number of optima is odd, into two groups one of which has one more optima than the other. Figure 4.3 shows one such line and a point, A, which is not on the line. If, from point A, we drop a perpendicular to the median line, then the point at the base of the perpendicular, A', will be closer to all the points on the other side of the line and the two points on the line than is A. It can, therefore, get a majority over A. Actually there would be a small lozenge, as in figure 4.3, outlining points which could get a majority over A. The geometry of this lozenge, however, will vary somewhat depending upon the exact location of the individual optima, so we will confine ourselves to the simple perpendicular relationship.

Figure 4.3

Most of these median lines would intersect in a tiny area in the center of the issue space. If we greatly magnified this area and drew in only a few of the median lines, we would get something which looked like figure 4.4. If we start with point A, then our theorem indicates that B can get a majority over it. C, on the other hand, can get a majority over B. Similarly, it is obvious that there

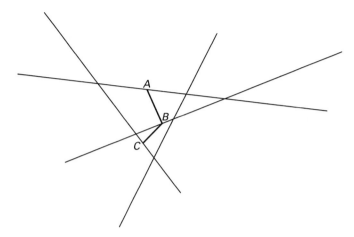

Figure 4.4

would be other points which can get majorities over C. Starting with any point in this general area, it will be possible to select points which will obtain a majority over it. Thus, there is no point which can get a majority over all other points.

The area in which the bulk of the bisectors intersect is, of course, very small, but in some cases the point of intersection might be far away from the center of the issue space. Suppose that there are an odd number of points and we select one which is near the extreme outer edge of the issue space. It may be possible to draw through this point two lines each of which pass through another point, and each of which divide the optima so that there is only one more on one side of the line than on the other. The angle between these two lines would be extremely small, but by exaggerating this angle we get the situation shown in figure 4.5. Above this pair of lines there would be 499,998 optima and below

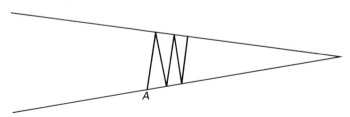

Figure 4.5

the same number. The three points lying on the lines make up our total of 999,999. If we start at any point on either of these lines, such as *A*, we can drop a perpendicular to the other and thus obtain a point which can get a majority over the first point. From this second point, we can then drop a perpendicular to the first line and obtain a point which can get a majority over it. By continuing this process we can eventually approach the intersection point which, by assumption, lies at the outer edge of our space. Thus it is possible, by simple majority voting, to reach points at almost any portion of the issue space. Needless to say, this sort of series of votes is highly unlikely. It can be easily recognized because it would involve a long series of votes in each of which there was only a one-vote difference between the majority and the minority. Since we never see this in the real world, we can feel reasonably confident that this type of movement away from the center does not occur.

Since standard voting procedures do not permit infinitely fine adjustment, the fact that majority voting would not lead to a unique solution seems of very little importance. Black defines a "majority motion" as a proposition "which is able to obtain a simple majority over all of the other motions concerned."[13] The rules of procedure make it unlikely that such a motion will be selected by majority voting. The outcome should be a motion which could not get a simple majority over *all* other motions, but only over those other motions which differ enough so that they can be put against it under the procedural rules. The result is an approximation, but a reasonably satisfactory one. Thus if there is no true majority motion, if endless cycling were the predicted outcome of efforts to obtain perfect adjustment, this would not change the outcome at all if the cycles would only involve motions proposing such small changes that they could be ruled out of order. Even if the cycles slightly enlarged the area in which the voting system was indeterminate, this would be a trivial defect. Only if the cycles would involve "moves" substantially larger than the minimum permitted by the procedural system would they be a significant problem.

The investigation of the likely size of cycles in the real world can proceed by making assumptions about the distribution of voters and rules of order and then calculating the likelihood of cycles among motions which differ enough so that they could be voted on, or by observing the real world.[14] There would seem to be two possible explanations for this paucity of examples of the phenomenon. Either it does not occur very commonly, which would be in accord with the theoretical considerations given above, or it is hard to detect the presence of cycles even when they are present.

In order to examine the possibility that the shortage of real world examples of cycles is explained not by their rarity, but by the difficulty of detecting them, let us consider the actual methods of voting used in most representative bodies. Under Robert's Rules, or the innumerable variants which exist, the procedure is quite complicated. We need not examine these rules in detail; a simplified generalization of them will suffice. Let us, therefore, examine the following system. A motion is made to move from the status quo. An amendment to this motion may then be proposed, and various subamendments to the amendment. All of the amendments and subamendments can be regarded as separate proposals. The distinguishing characteristic of this sytem is that a whole set of proposals is made before any of them are voted upon, and then that they are voted upon in a fixed order which is known in advance.

Suppose that the status quo is *A*. *B* is offered as a motion. *C* would be offered only if its sponsor thought it could beat both *A* and *B*. (Or, in special circumstances, if it might lead to a blocking cycle. This will be discussed below.) But people do make mistakes. Let us suppose, then, that someone in error offers amendment *C*. This is followed by subamendment *D*, which has been correctly calculated and can beat *A*, *B*, and *C*. For our purposes, we may use a simple set of rules providing that motions, amendments, and subamendments are voted upon in reverse order from that in which they are proposed. Thus *D* would be put against *C*, would win; would be put against *B*, and would win; and then would be put against the status quo, *A*, and win again. Note that *C*, the miscalculation, has no effect on the voting except to delay it slightly. Such mistakes will certainly be made; hope springs eternal in the human breast, but they have no effect on the outcome. We can, therefore, ignore them.

Let us now consider the possibility of cycles. In figure 4.6, we start with the status quo at *A*. Suppose that a motion, *B*, were

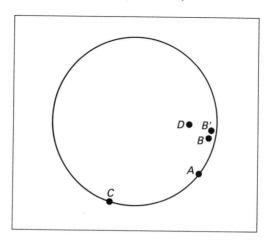

Figure 4.6

introduced which could beat *A*. Either by accident, or by calculation, another motion *C*, might be introduced which could beat *B*, but would be beaten by *A*. Deliberate contrivance of such a cycle by people who prefer *A* to *B* but realize that *B* would win in a direct confrontation would be rational. The existence of a cycle, of course, does not prevent other amendments from being offered. *D*, for example, could beat any member of the cycle.

If, however, *D* were not offered, the voting on *C*, *B*, and *A* would not immediately lead to an apparent cycle because *A* would be chosen if they were voted on in the order specified. This type of concealed cycle, however, should not lead to a stable result. Once the voting has led to a return to the status quo, further proposals for change would be strongly urged. If there were strict rules forbidding the reintroduction of a measure which had been voted down,[15] then some other proposal, say *B'*, would be offered. We could expect to see essentially the same series of proposals and amendments retraced again and again. The absence of this kind of repetition in actual legislative practice is evidence that there are few concealed cycles in real world legislative activity.

So far we have been mostly concerned with the situation when there are only two variables and they are continuous. The generalization of the conclusions to many-dimensional issue space is obvious, but the effect of shifting to a noncontinuous variable

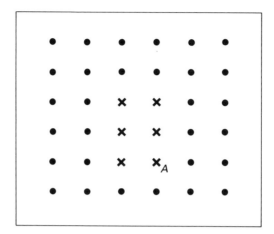

Figure 4.7

may not be. In figure 4.7 we show a situation where the two variables are both discontinuous, and hence only certain points in the issue space are possible. The principal difference which this restriction makes is that there are now far fewer points which can get a majority over some given point. Point *A*, for example, is dominated only by the six points marked with *X*'s. The likelihood that one of the points that dominate *A* is equally or farther distant from the center than *A*, is reduced when the total number of points is small, and the likelihood that there will be a set of points which are in a cycle is small. The tiny central area where every point is dominated by some other is apt to be nonexistent simply because there are two few points in this region. On the other hand, cycles are only unlikely, not impossible. If a cycle does occur, it is likely to be of more than trivial significance if the distances between the points are sizable and the cycle must, therefore, involve sizable differences of policy. In sum, with discontinuous issue space, cycles must be rare but are apt to be important when they occur.

Our discussion so far has been based upon a special type of interdependence of the preference structures of individuals. It is assumed that social states, products, and laws differ in a number of characteristics.[16] Each of these characteristics may be arranged along an axis, either as a continuous variable or as a series of points. Each individual is assumed to have some optimum point in the resulting dimensional space, and it is assumed that the individual's degree of satisfaction falls off as we move away from his optima in any direction. This later assumption, in the form of perfectly circular indifference curves,[17] is too strong, and we shall shortly demonstrate that a weaker assumption will do as well. Similarly, our assumption of even distribution of the optima over the issue space is a simpliyfing assumption which will shortly be dropped. Leaving these two issues aside, however, the general picture should raise few objections from economists. Special cases in which these conditions do not hold can be invented, but most choice problems will arise in environments which lead to this sort of preference system. The fact that each person has a preference structure of this sort, together with the fact that they are all in the same hyper-space gives them a rather probable type of interdependence, and our conclusions are essentially derived from this interdependence. Note, however, the rather special form of this interdependence. My preferences do not in any way affect yours. The interdependence comes solely from the fact that we are choosing from among the same set of alternatives and these alternatives are such that they restrict the form of our preference structures in a way which leads to our conclusion.

So far we have used two unrealistic assumptions, that the indifference curves are all perfect circles, and that the individual optima are evenly distributed over the issue space. The elimination of these assumptions will make the model much more realistic. Let us being by considering more realistic distributions of the optima.[18] Presumably the common distribution is to have the optima arranged in a bell-shaped distribution with its peak somewhere in the issue space. This distribution raises no particular problem for our demonstration. The "median lines" could still be constructed, and they would still mostly intersect near the peak of the distribution. This would mean that the same tendency to move to a small area in the center would exist. Similarly, a skewed normal distribution would raise no particular difficulties, although the point where most median lines intersected would not necessarily be at the peak of the distribution.

Multi-peaked distributions raise more difficulties, although the only clear cases leading to significant cycles which I have been able to produce involve extreme degrees of multi-peakedness. As an example, if the optima are arranged in three discrete groups arranged in a triangle, as figure 4.8, and roughly a third of them are in each group, then cycling would occur over an area of significant size. The general difficulty of finding such phenomena can, perhaps, be illustrated by the fact that division of the optima into four roughly equal groups does not lead to significant cycles.

The elimination of the assumption that the indifference curves are perfect circles raises no particular difficulties if large numbers of people are involved in the decision process. Arrow wrote his book about the problem of selecting a "social welfare function" and this clearly would involve many millions of individuals. In the more general problems of collective choice, there also normally are enough individual preferences to be "aggregated" so that the law of large numbers can be applied. Granted large numbers of individuals,[19] any reasonable preference structure will aggregate in more or less the same way as our perfect circles. On the average, and with large numbers of voters, the average is what counts, of majority voting will choose the alternative which is closest to the optima of the majority of the voters. Suppose, for example, that we have two groups of 1,000,000 voters, A and B. Assume that of two alternatives X and Y, X lies closer to the optima of all members of Group A, and Y closer to the optima of all members of group B. We would expect about 1,000,000 votes for X and about

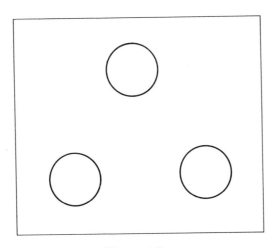

Figure 4.8

1,000,000 for Y if that choice were put to the 2,000,000 voters even if 100,000 voters in group A had preference mountains which were so shaped that they preferred Y to X. This would be so because the law of large numbers would indicate, lacking some special phenomenon, that there would also be about 100,000 voters in group B who preferred X to Y.

Note, however, that we only get an approximate result here. With the voters evenly divided, the small random variation which we would expect would decide the election. If the numbers in the two groups differed by more than the likely random variation, however, the outcome would not be affected. Thus the introduction of what amounts to a stochastic variable by considering indifference curves which are not perfect circles blurs our conclusions a little, and expands the small area in the center of the distribution in which cycles can occur by a small amount, but does not basically alter our conclusions.

That the majority voting process normally leads to a determinate outcome and that this outcome is apt to be reasonably satisfactory will surprise no practical man. Clearly this is what does happen. One of the real problems raised by Arrow's book was why the real world democracies seemed to function fairly well in spite of the logical impossibility of rationally aggregating preferences. The solution I have offered, that no decision process will meet Arrow's criteria perfectly, but that a very common decision process meets them to a very high degree of approximation, permits us to reconcile the theoretical impossibility with the practical success of democracy.

5

Social Cost and Government Action

In Illinois where I was born – and indeed in most of the two American continents – the common mosquito is a major pest. With the development of DDT during World War II, a cheap way of reducing the mosquito population became available, and a very large number of communities in the years after World War II hired aircraft to fly low over the city and spray it with DDT. Recently this has become much less common. The reduction in the amount of such spraying is partially the result of a realization that the DDT spray has other effects on the natural environment than the reduction of the mosquitoes, and that some of these other effects may be quite undesirable, and partially the result of home air conditioning. A person living in an air-conditioned home is unlikely to spend as much time outside as a person living in a non-air-conditioned house. Although the amount of aerial spraying of mosquitoes has been considerably reduced in recent years, a number of other techniques which are both less effective in dealing with mosquitoes and more expensive have been adopted in some areas. They are not as widespread as aerial spraying was, let us say, ten or 15 years ago.

The reader may wonder why a discussion of social cost should begin with this technological discussion of a rather unusual local problem. The reason is simple. Almost all of the problems involved in decisions as to what types of activity should be undertaken by the government will be found in this simple example. Further, there is absolutely nothing in the way of a traditional solution to this problem. One of the greatest problems in talking about the new discoveries in the field of social cost, externalities, and what we might call the economics of the government sector is that most people have learned, normally very early in life, the existing tradition. Those who have not accepted the existing tradition normally learn some particular attack on it which is in many ways just another tradition. Thus discussion of government activities runs instantaneously into a barrier of very strongly held ideas. If we discuss mosquito abatement, however, we normally find a complete absence of these traditions or antitraditions and hence can deal with the problem with less emotional difficulty.

To return, then, to the mosquitoes, let us assume that we are in 1952 and that we are living in a small town in Iowa where our mosquito problem is bad. We could undertake a spraying campaign in our own backyard. We could buy in a local supermarket a suitable insect spray and spray our backyard and perhaps spray a little into the neighbor's yard. This spray would in general reduce the number of mosquitoes in the area, partly by killing the ones who were there at the time we sprayed and partly because the spray left some residuum on the vegetation and mosquitoes landing on the residuum might be killed. Nevertheless, this would be a very expensive and not tremendously efficient way of reducing the number of mosquitoes.

Another method of mosquito abatement was available, however; for $50.00 we could hire an airplane and this would spray the entire town with a density to give me or any other citizen considerable mosquito abatement. This method, like the use of handsprays, could be intensified with additional deaths of mosquitoes. The situation is shown in figure 5.1. For some individual the demand for mosquito abatement is shown by the usual slanting line. If he chooses to use the handspray method, then the line marked $1.00 will indicate the cost of killing "one unit" of mosquitoes. The individual will choose to purchase A units, and the total cost he will run for this will be represented by the rectangle to the left of A. The individual will not be interested in hiring an airplane which, from the standpoint of the individual, is completely dominated by handspraying. He can obtain any amount of mosquito abatement in his own yard that he desires more cheaply by handspraying than from the air.

The situation changes radically, however, if the individual clubs

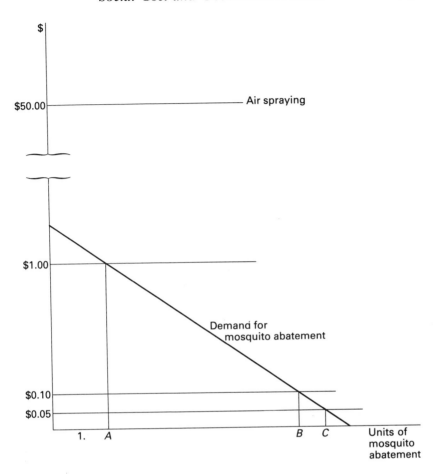

Figure 5.1

together with the other citizens of the town to hire the airplane. Suppose there are 1,000 citizens in the town and they get together to hire the plane. The cost to each of them for mosquito abatement in his backyard falls to five cents a unit and the total amount consumed would rise to C. Under these circumstances the entire mosquito abatement demand would be taken up by air spraying rather than handspraying because, once again, there is strict dominance of this particular technological method.

Clearly, the individual, if given a choice, would prefer C mosquito abatement by air spraying to consuming A units by handspray. Thus there would be a good argument for collective provision of mosquito abatement. Suppose, however, that instead of having some government instrumentality undertake mosquito abatement, an effort is made to have various individuals privately contribute money to hire an airplane. Under these circumstances the cost of hiring an airplane depends on the number of people who have contributed. If only 500 people are willing to contribute, then the cost of mosquito abatement by air (per unit) would be ten cents and they will choose to purchase the amount *B*.

Assuming that this voluntary method of purchasing mosquito abatement is adopted, the individual would be rational not to make his ten cent payment. If he is not a member of the group making the payment, he receives the mosquito abatement free. If, on the other hand, he decides to make his payment and we assume that the amount of money he puts in is then invested in purchasing additional aircraft time for the whole city, then he faces a price for puchasing mosquito abatement in his yard of $50.00 a unit. This price is clearly way above the amount that he wishes to pay. It is extremely unlikely that individuals would be willing to make voluntary contributions. Normally only a government could provide the airplane spraying.[1]

We thus have what appears to be a fairly unambiguous argument for a governmental agency compelling the citizens of this small town to make the five cent payments for the hire of an airplane. The citizens themselves would be better off under this arrangement and would presumably favor it. There has, however, been an implicit assumption in the discussion so far – which is that each of the citizens has exactly the same demand for mosquito abatement. Presumably, this is not true. This means that a decision must be made as to how much mosquito abatement should be purchased. In order to consider this decision, let us shift to figure 5.2 in which we show the demand curves for mosquito abatement of three citizens (Mr A, Mr B, and Mr C). Note that if there is no decision to hire an airplane, the three individuals will simply purchase different numbers of units of mosquito abatement through the use of the handspray: Mr A purchasing a' units, Mr B purchasing b' units, and Mr C purchasing c' units.

If, however, it is decided to hire an airplane and engage in collective provision of mosquito abatement, then some kind of decision must be made as to how much mosquito abatement should be purchased. It will be noted that the three individuals have different ideas as to how much this should be – represented by *a*, *b*, and *c* on the diagram. I have carefully constructed this example so that their preferences on this particular point would be what is known as "single peaked."[2] If we consider ourselves as dealing with only a three-person community and they make decisions by majority voting, and in this particular type of situation there are arguments for doing this, then we would predict that they would purchase the amount *b* of mosquito

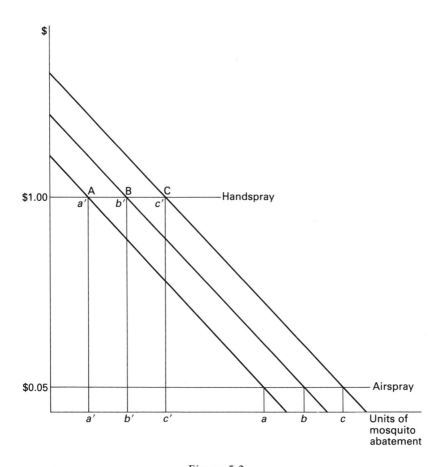

Figure 5.2

abatement. This means that Mr A and Mr C have failed to obtain their optimum amount of mosquito abatement.

It does not, of course, follow from the fact that the individuals could make a perfect adjustment of how much mosquito abatement they wish to purchase if we use handsprays and must anticipate in most cases that they will not obtain their exact optimum amount of mosquito abatement if we use airplanes to spray, that handspraying is superior. It merely follows that there is a cost involved in the air spraying which should be taken into account. Assuming again that we have our society of 1,000, I would compare my desire for handsprays (that is, how much I would purchase in the way of mosquito abatement by hand) which what I thought was the likely outcome of the voting process in terms of the amount which would be obtained by collective provision. I would anticipate that the collective provision would not turn out to be exactly the amount that I wanted at that price. It would not follow from this that I would favor exact adjustment under what we might call market provision to imperfect adjustment under collective arrangements. Indeed, I presume most people in areas where mosquitoes are bad if confronted with the particular problem that I have outlined would choose the collective provision. Note, however, that this means that they are choosing a less than optimal arrangement of the resources by their own preference ordering. There is, in a sense, an externality imposed upon them by the choice of the collective decision process. They will no longer be able to make an ideal adjustment.

Let us now inquire what is the ideal size of the government unit which deals with mosquito abatement. First, we should note the limits that are placed upon this by the technology of aircraft spraying. In order to be efficient, the aircraft should spray the entire town and certain nearby mosquito breeding areas. An effort to spray half of the town would give much less than half the protection. In other words, it would be a very bad bargain. Therefore, the minimum size of government units which decides to hire the airplane would be our small town in the Middle West.

By rather similar methods we can determine the maximum size of government units for mosquito abatement. In general every increase in the size of the unit reduces the likelihood that the final provision will be very close to the desires of a given citizen. This is particularly true in something like mosquito abatement where different communities presumably have different levels of mosquito infestation. In general, as the size of government units is increased the number of externalities internalized is increased but the adjustment of the government activity to the desires of any individual voter is decreased. In our particular case, mosquito abatement, the laying off of these two factors leads pretty unambiguously to the view that the small Iowa community should provide its own mosquito abatement. With other problems, of course, other solutions should be expected.

So far, we have been talking about the problem of mosquito abatement about ten years ago. There has been considerable technological change since that time. Let us confine ourselves to considering only those discoveries which indicate that simple airplane spraying of DDT is not a desirable way of dealing with the problem. It has been realized that there are a large number of secondary costs from this operation and that these secondary costs may well be much in excess of the benefit to the spraying process. As a result, the technology of mosquito abatement no longer mainly depends on this very cheap method of killing mosquitoes. We need not go into the more complicated and more expensive methods that are now in general use. It is perfectly possible that tomorrow someone will invent another method of getting rid of mosquitoes that is as cheap as aerial spraying of DDT was thought to be when it was widely used, but we can simply note that present methods are expensive and inquire what effect this would have on the reasoning so far.

The first possible effect of the increase in expense of mosquito abatement by collective measures might be that the unit cost of a given amount of mosquito abatement by collective measures would be equal or higher than if one restricts mosquito abatement to the private use of sprays in one own backyard. In this case, which is an easy one, the proper decision of course would be to abandon completely all collective efforts to reduce mosquitoes. The second possibility (also very easy) is that mosquito abatement either by public or by private means might become so expensive that it would be no longer desired by individuals. Here, again, the proper solution is to have no public program for mosquito abatement, and we would also anticipate that there would be no private abatement either. Both of these are easy problems and in both cases we need go no further with our analysis.

The interesting question, however, is what would we do if the use of various public means for reducing the mosquito population (let us say, specialized treatment of breeding areas of mosquitoes) is still a less expensive method of obtaining a certain amount of mosquito abatement than is private spraying, but that the difference becomes small. On figure 5.3 I have drawn in this problem.

We assume here that methods of mosquito abatement by collective means exist and these are efficient enough so that if all members of the community are compelled to contribute the cost of purchasing one unit of mosquito abatement it will be $0.95 per head, whereas private purchase of one unit of mosquito abatement would remain at $1.00. If we consider only Mr B, clearly collective provisions would be desirable. He would be better off purchasing x units of mosquito abatement at $0.95 instead of purchasing b units at $1.00 which is his market economy alternative. His net benefit is measured by the areas shaded horizontally and slanting to the left in figure 5.3.

If, however, we consider a community consisting of three members (Mr A, Mr B, and Mr C), the situation is more complicated. Mr A, for example, benefits from the establishment of the new level of mosquito abatement to the extent of the horizontally shaded trapezoid in the upper left. He is injured through the necessity of buying more mosquito abatement than he wants even at the new price to the extent of the vertically shaded triangle. Clearly, he is much worse off with collective provision than he would be with individual provision. Mr C is affected in a somewhat more ambiguous way. His gross gain is the gross gain of Mr B plus the little dotted triangle. He, however, suffers a loss to the extent of the shaded triangle from not being able to purchase the additional mosquito abatement privately. This loss will only be suffered if it is not possible for him (for technological or for legal reasons) to supplement the public provision at the same cost as he could have bought mosquito abatement privately before. If the public provision of mosquito abatement actually reduced the cost of additional mosquito abatement (which is conceivable), he might gain. If the public provision did not completely bar private but

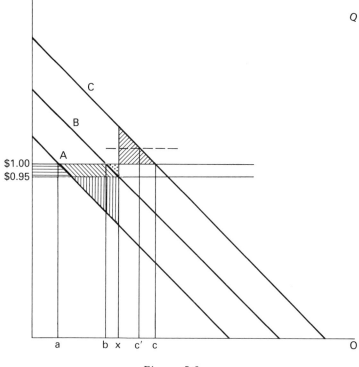

Figure 5.3

simply made private supplement rather inefficient (which I imagine is the common case), then Mr C would face a supply curve somewhat like the horizontal dashed line and would purchase $c' - x$ amount of private mosquito abatement. The gross cost to him of the new arrangement then would be the trapezoid lying between this horizontal dashed line and the $1.00 line. If this were a smaller area than the rectangle to the left of the new supply quantity, he would gain in net terms.

Now the question arises naturally whether it would be desirable to undertake public provision of the mosquito abatement granted that we have this small three-person community. If the provision of public mosquito abatement injures both Mr A and Mr C and benefits Mr B, then the ordinary welfare ecnomist can inquire whether Mr B is able to compensate Mr A and Mr C for this injury. If (and this is also quite possible) the provision benefits both Mr B and Mr C but injures Mr A, then, of course, it will be more likely that compensation can be undertaken. Unfortunately, when we are talking about public goods and where the quantity of public good consumed is set by voting or any other collective process, compensation becomes almost impossible in the real world.

The problem is that we will be unable to find out the amount of the compensation. Mr A probably has not given much thought to how much he would require to compensate him for a combination of x provision collectively and the appropriate taxes. If asked to give thought to this rather strange problem, he has absolutely no motive to correctly interpret his own feelings. This would be particularly true if we were dealing not with our small three-man community. Mr A might be concerned with the prospect that too large a claim for damages on his part might make the whole project impossible. Thus, there will be some limit to the degree to which he would exaggerate the loss which he would suffer. Similarly, Mr B and Mr C even if they are benefited probably would be hard pressed to put a monetary value on their benefit if we asked them and have substantially no motive to do so accurately.

As a general principle, attempting to get voters voting on some issue to compensate each other out of their individual surpluses for their individual losses is not a feasible political proposition. Thus, we cannot use the traditional welfare economics method of making a direct payment from the people who gain to the people who were injured. There is, however, another and rather debatable tool in the welfare economist's tool kit. Some (but by no means all) welfare economists would argue that if we could compute that the payment would be possible, then it is not necessary to make it. Under this line of reasoning if there is a net social benefit, we don't need to concern ourselves with the way in which it is distributed. This method of applying the Paretian criterion is controverial and I do not wish to endorse it here. There is, however, a variant on it which is clearly a respectable rule and one which we will use.

According to this variant, if we anticipate making a large number of decisions in the future and if we cannot tell who will be benefited and who will be injured by each of these collective decisions but anticipate that most members of the society will find themselves benefited sometimes and injured sometimes, then the rule of simply computing whether there is a net benefit or not and using that for all of these decisions would probably give to each individual in society a positive discounted future income stream. It could be said under this argument that if we found a "net gain" we could undertake the collective provision of mosquito abatement without worrying about the fact that some people (particularly Mr A) are injured. It will be noted that the use of this argument involves an income transfer. Mr A is injured, Mr B is benefited, and depending on the particular parameters of the problem Mr C may be either benefited or injured. This transfer is clearly not something we would positively favor. That is particularly true since as a general rule most members of society who are interested in restricting the consumption of any particular good are apt to be poorer members. Thus transfers of the sort we are now talking about are apt to be transfers from the poorer to the better-off members of the community. Poor Mr A is made worse off, middle-class Mr B is benefited and upper-class Mr C may gain.

It will be noted that the basic parameters which have led us to choose either collective or private provision of mosquito abatement have been essentially technological. It is, therefore, sensible to pause briefly and inquire exactly what the nature of technological superiority of collective provision is. At first glance, one might think that it was simply an example of an ordinary scale economy, but this is clearly not so. General Motors has surely exhausted all the scale economies that are available in the manufacture of Chevrolets, yet we find no need for collective provision here. General Motors can sell its cars to people scattered all over the United States without worrying very much about whether the next-door neighbor of any given purchaser of Chevrolet has a Ford.

The special characteristic of aerial spraying of mosquitoes is that it is generally impossible to do it economically on one city lot at a time. In order to get any economy into the operation at all it is necessary to spray a fairly broad area. This is partly because the plane must fly from its airport to the place where it releases the spray anyway and partly that the characteristics of the spray are such that it is apt to cover several surrounding house lots anyway. If only one of them is paying for it, the others will receive a free ride. The problem, then, is geographical contiguity. Geographical contiguity is a basic characteristic of almost all such areas where we would choose collective provision. The distinction between any economy of scale which can be obtained only if the customers are located next door to each other and an economy of scale which can be obtained without this type of contiguity is fundamental.

6

A Simple Algebraic Logrolling Model

In the rapidly developing literature in which essentially economic tools are applied to political problems, there have been two major models of voting performance. One of the models, by all odds the most widely used, is essentially spatial. In it, individuals are assumed to have a preference mountain and to prefer the points which are closer to their optimum to points which are farther away. This model, which started as a very simple one-dimensional continuum in the work of Harold Hotelling, Duncan Black, and Anthony Downs,[1] has developed into a more complex, many dimensional model in the later work of Black, Otto Davis and M. J. Hinich, and Tullock.[2] The many dimensional version of this model must be represented, of course, by some variant on the Cartesian algebra since it is not easy to represent graphically more than two dimensions on a piece of paper. In general, these models have been used mainly to demonstrate that in a two-party system, the two parties will normally have platforms that are very similar and that these will represent median preferences. The other model deals with the phenomenon of logrolling and has normally been represented by other tools.[3] The interrelation between these two models has been discussed in general by Davis and Hinich and Tullock,[4] but no very rigorous joint model exists. It is the purpose of this article to demonstrate that the two approaches are not inconsistent by presenting a spatial model which will also cover logrolling.

Three-Person Model

Suppose that an individual must choose government policies with respect to three different issues which we shall designate A, B, and C, and that each of these issues represents a continuum, such as the appropriation for the army or the appropriation for the welfare program. This situation can be represented by a three-dimensional issue space with each of the issues representing one dimension and an individual having some point which is for him optimal, let us say [10, 10, 10]. Presumably his level of satisfaction will fall off as the actual social choice moves away from his optimum. If we assume that this fall-off is uniform in every direction, we may express his loss from not achieving his optimum by the equation:

$$L_A^2 = [A - 10]^2 + [B - 10]^2 + [C - 10]^2 \qquad (6.1)$$

If we had a number of people with varying optima in the issue space, we would be able to deduce from the resulting set of equations similar to equation (6.1) how they would vote on each proposition that was put before them.[5] As has been demonstrated by the spatial models so far published, except with very special distributions of optima, the outcome under simple majority voting would be some point which is approximately at the median of the entire distribution. This conclusion is readily generalizable up to any number of issues, since the Cartesian system can be applied to an issue space of any number of dimensions.

The use of perfectly spherical indifference surfaces in this model does not appear to restrict its utility very much. In the real world, we would not anticipate such perfection, but the deviations from it would be essentially random and the law of large numbers should lead, where there are many voters, to much the same outcome as if we used our spheres.[6] Systematic deviations from the spherical model, together with appropriately structured locations of the individual optima, could lead to voting cycles, and the conclusion that the median preference dominates would be undermined. It is the purpose of this article to consider an important case in which we would anticipate that the individual indifference curves would systematically vary from the spherical in a particular way, and in which we would anticipate that individual preferences would have a structure such that the combination of these two effects leads to quite different results than have customarily been dealt with by the spatial models.

If we consider those situations in the real world in which we observe logrolling and compare them with those situations where logrolling appears to be relatively unimportant, we observe immediate differences in the structure of the individual preferences. In logrolling, we observe a number of people who are highly interested in one particular project, let us say, the dredging of the James so that Richmond becomes a deep-water port, and only mildly interested in other projects which, generally speaking, they oppose. The rivers and harbors area is the *locus classicus* of logrolling, but similar phenomena will be found throughout a very large part of modern governments.

The indifference curves of the individuals engaging in logrolling are somewhat similar to those shown in figure 6.1. Mr A wants his harbor dredged at the expense of the general taxpayer and feels quite strongly about it, but he would rather not pay for dredging Mr B's harbor. Since he is only one of many taxpayers, however, his feeling about the dredging of Mr B's harbor is much feebler than his feeling about his own. Mr B's feelings are the converse. If we assume that all of the citizens of the town in which Mr A lives feel much the same as Mr A[7] and the other citizens of the town in which Mr B lives feel much the same as Mr B, then logrolling becomes rational. Point C is better than the origin for both Mr A and Mr B. It is not, however, possible to represent a many-dimensional logrolling process in two dimensions and, if we consider such a piece of legislation as the rivers and harbors bill, it is clear that several thousand dimensions would be necessary.

We can begin with a simple three-dimensional model using the ordinary Cartesian algebra. This model for logrolling will differ from the usual spatial model only in that the individuals are assumed to have intense preferences on certain subjects. If we assume a three-person society where harbor dredging is paid for by equal per capita taxes, and that there are three harbor dredging operations contemplated (A, B, and C), then Mr A's preferences can be represented by the first equation in table 6.1. Mr A is assumed to have his personal optimum at the point $[10, 0, 0]$. L_A is the "loss" he suffers if the government chooses some other point. As in the real world, he is much more interested in the dredging of his own harbor than in preventing the dredging of the other two harbors, although he doesn't like paying taxes to benefit other people. Note that Mr A's optima includes his own per capita share in terms of tax payments for his own harbor. For simplicity we will continue to assume throughout that all expenditures on logrolled projects are paid for by a tax which is evenly divided among the taxpayers and the per capita cost is our metric on each issue dimension.

Logrolling Results

Taken on the two dimensions represented by axes *A* and *B* and holding *C* equal to zero, the indifference curves generated by the equations of *A* and *B* in the positive quadrant will approximate those shown in figure 6.1. In three dimensions, *A*'s indifference surfaces in the positive part of the issue space would form a quarter of a disk with its center at the point [10, 0, 0]. The other three individuals in our current simple model would have similar

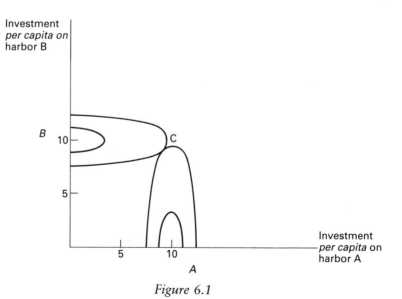

Figure 6.1

disks attached to the other three axes. If the voting rule is simple majority voting, and each individual votes for his preference on each of the three harbor proposals, then there will be two votes against each proposal and all will fail. L_A would equal 22.4. The individuals, however, should notice the possibility for gains from trade. If two of them could get together and vote for each other's harbor dredging project, then they can make a quite considerable gain. Bargaining difficulties in this case are apt to be minimal since each party to the bargain has the alternative of turning to the third party and hence in essence they are operating in a market-type situation.[8] Thus, if we assume that there is some agreement between Mr A and Mr B and that they choose an equal amount of harbor dredging in each of their harbors,[9] it's fairly easy to determine the point in the issue space which would result. It is [8⅓, 8⅓, 0]. L_A and L_B will be 9.1,[10] very much better than the situation without the agreement. L_C, on the other hand, is now 27.2, much worse than the situation before the agreement was made. The reason, of course, is simple. Mr C's harbor is not being dredged and he is paying taxes to dredge the other two.

TABLE 6.1

$$L_A^2 = 5(A - 10)^2 + B^2 + C^2$$
$$L_B^2 = A^2 + 5(B - 10)^2 + C^2$$
$$L_C^2 = A^2 + B^2 + 5(C - 10)^2$$

This may be taken as a very simple example of the type of bargain which occurs in logrolling. In practice, things are more complicated. There are basically two types of logrolling. The first is explicit logrolling, most often observed in Congress although it does occur in other situations. It involves individuals who trade their votes on many individual issues to many others for votes on other issues. Under these circumstances, there is no reason why any particular person would be left out. Everyone may trade with anyone else and the result amounts of a peculiar market solution. Since in making the trades, each individual is only attempting to make up a majority coalition, the cost calculations are similar to those informing the agreement we just discussed. Nevertheless, the fact that everyone may get their project means the outcome is different.[11] With just three voters this result would not occur, but with more voters the outcome of this process might well be that all of the harbors would be dredged at a level equivalent to $8\frac{1}{3}$.[12] The individual is in marginal adjustment on those logrolling deals in which he has participated and loses on those in which he has not. L_A, assuming that all three harbors are dredged to the level of expenditure of $8\frac{1}{3}$, is 12.3. This is worse than Mr A obtains from his simple agreement with Mr B, but it is certainly much better than he would obtain if no agreements were made at all.

The other type of logrolling is called implicit logrolling and involves political parties or candidates who present "platforms." These platforms, in essence, are complex mixes of different measures. A proposal to dredge two of three harbors would be an example of such a platform. Assuming that this type of logrolling is adopted then the individual *ex ante* has two chances out of three of being a member of the coalition and having his harbor dredged, and one chance in three of having to pay taxes for the dredging of two other harbors. Discounting this out in a simple manner, L_A *ex ante* would be 15.1. Once again, it is much better than a no-logrolling solution. Unfortunately, this type of solution is not mathematically stable, but we will defer discussion of the matter, closely related to Arrow's general impossibility theorem, until the latter part of this article.

So far, we have said nothing about Pareto optimality. If we require unanimity, clearly the bargaining costs would be high, but the economists would normally anticipate that the ultimate outcome, if we disregard the bargaining costs, would be better than the outcomes obtained by partial agreement. The Pareto optimal area is, of course, quite a complex surface running across the three-dimensional space. We can, however, fairly easily compute the value of one particular point on that surface. With our highly symmetric model, side payments would lead to a decision to dredge all three harbors equally at $7\frac{1}{7}$ each and the loss function of that point to Mr A would be 11.8. *Ex ante* the side payments would cancel out and this is better than any of the other possibilities we have discussed. Needless to say, for an individual who can feel sure that he will be one of a pair of voters who have only their harbors dredged, that outcome would be better than the Pareto optimal outcome.

Five Voters

The method of calculation we have been describing can readily be applied to any number of dimensions. For example, asssume that there are five harbors and five voters (groups and voters) whose loss functions are as shown in table 6.2. Once again, if all the projects for dredging habors are put up individually and all the individuals vote on them strictly in accordance with their preference on each issue, in each case there will be four votes against and one in favor. The resulting outcome will be the origin of the five-dimensional Cartesian axis system and L_A will be again 22.4. If we assume that three groups of voters, those on harbors, A, B, and C, get together to form a majority, they would agree to vote for $[7\frac{1}{7}, 7\frac{1}{7}, 7\frac{1}{7}, 0, 0]$. This gives L_A equal to 12.0, much better than would be obtained without bargaining. Messrs D and E, not members of the winning coalition in this case, however, find that the payoff of 25.6 is worse than would have been obtained had logrolling not existed.

TABLE 6.2

$$L_A^2 = 5(A - 10)^2 + B^2 + C^2 + D^2 + E^2$$
$$L_B^2 = A^2 + 5(B - 10)^2 + C^2 + D^2 + E^2$$
$$L_C^2 = A^2 + B^2 + 5(C - 10)^2 + D^2 + E^2$$
$$L_D^2 = A^2 + B^2 + C^2 + 5(D - 10)^2 + E^2$$
$$L_E^2 = A^2 + B^2 + C^2 + D^2 + 5(E - 10)^2$$

Using our group of five, however, we can consider a variety of voting rules. Table 6.3 shows on the left the minimum size of the coalition which is required by various voting rules. The outcome in terms of the amount of dredging in each harbor is shown in the second vertical column, the third column shows the payoff to a member of the winning coalition, and the fourth, the payoff to a man who is left out. In the final column, we show the *ex ante* value of the arrangement for some person who does not know whether he will be a winner or a loser but who assumes his probability of being in the winning coalition is proportional to the number of people required. For comparison purposes, we have put the no-logrolling outcome at the bottom of the table.

TABLE 6.3

Minimum coalition size	Platform	Payoff to member of winning coalition	Payoff to nonmember	Ex ante Payoff
2	8⅓,8⅓,0,0,0	9.1	27.2	19.9
3	7½,7½,7½,0,0,	12.0	25.6	17.4
4	6¼,6¼,6¼,6¼,0	13.7	25.6	16.1
5	5⁵⁄₉,5⁵⁄₉,5⁵⁄₉,5⁵⁄₉,5⁵⁄₉	15.0	—	15.0
No logrolling	0, 0, 0, 0, 0			

The reader may be surprised at the existence of a voting rule permitting a coalition of two to obtain the dredging of their harbors. It is not, however, an unrealistic situation. Most modern democracies use a representative assembly. Under these circumstances, a majority of the voters in a majority of the constituencies may be able to control the outcome. Thus, less than a majority of the voters is necessary. Our two-voter coalition is an example.[13]

It will be noted that the numerical outcomes we have obtained from our simple calculation procedure are in exactly the form which would have been predicted from the nonnumerical discussion in Buchanan and Tullock. The costs of coalition formation, of course, must be offset against the numbers in table 6.3 to find the optimal voting rule. The point of this model has not been to advance the line of reasoning started in Buchanan and Tullock. Instead it provides a basis for future research by demonstrating that it is possible to obtain their conclusions through a model which differs from the widely used spatial models only by a minor change in parameters.

The outstanding characteristic of the type of issue that normally involves logrolling as opposed to the type of issue that normally does not, is simply that there are groups of voters who feel much more strongly about one particular issue than about others, and that these different groups of voters are arranged roughly in the symmetrical way that we have shown. Needless to say, the perfect symmetry which I have given the model is an aid to calculation, not an effort to describe the real world.

Other Models

In order to move from the model we have here to the type of model that was used in Davis and Hinich and Tullock,[14] we may begin by assuming that the individuals favor all of the goods provided to some extent. Suppose for example, that individual A's preferences for the dredging of harbor B is not simply an aversion to taxation for this purpose but that he actually does think it would be nice to have it dredged. Under these circumstances, the center of the disk which now describes his loss function would be moved away from the A-axis a short distance and corresponding computations would indicate that there would be somewhat more dredging of harbor B. This could also lead to the ellipse being shorter and fatter. In the limit, if we continue such operations, we would end with a circle with its center somewhere near the middle of the issue space.

However, we do not have to change our loss functions from disks to spheres in order to obtain approximately the results obtained by the analysis which shows the central policy is dominant. All that is necessary is to relax our extremely strict restrictions upon the shape of individual preferences. We have grouped the individuals in clusters along the axes very strongly favoring certain projects which benefit them and being opposed, mainly because of the tax cost, to individual projects of the same nature in other areas. This is, indeed, a very tight restriction. Unfortunately, it would appear that it is very commonly met in the real world. If we assume that this type of clustering does not occur, then we are back in the world of Davis and Hinich, and Tullock. Thus, we have obtained logrolling essentially out of the spatial model simply by assuming that there are people with the type of preference that we observe in logrolling situations.

So far, however, we have assumed that our function is stable. In actual fact, what we have referred to as explicit logrolling is indeed a stable situation, but, what we have called implicit is not. For example, if we return to the set of equations in table 6.1, the platform [10, 10, 0] can be beaten by the platform [10, 0, 0] which can be beaten by [0, 0, 0] which in turn can be beaten by [10, 10, 0]. Further, [10, 10, 0], [0, 10, 10], [10, 0, 10] are all possible winning outcomes. In my *Towards a Mathematics of Politics*, I argued that the instability (implied by the Arrow theorem) in respect to voting was of little real importance. My demonstration, however, depended on the assumption that the number of voters was very much in excess of the number of issue dimensions. When the votes are clustered well out on each of the issue dimensions as they are in our logrolling model, the proof that I offer ceases to be relevant. In essence, each cluster of voters acts as one voter and the number of such clusters is the same as the number of issue dimensions.

Applications

In the real world, voting would appear to cover many issues in which the preferences of the individual voters do not have the high degree of structure required for logrolling issues. The classical solution for such a problem for a party wishing to maximize votes would be to seek the middle position on the nonlogrolling issues, and on the logrolling issues, attempt to seize a position which is superior to whatever his opponent has offered. This would lead to sharp changes of policy and great differences between the two parties. We do not observe either of these things in the real world.

It should be noted that a good deal of the logrolling actually done in Congress is on an explicit basis rather than by the parties on an implicit basis. Both the Republican and Democratic congressional candidates from Richmond will be in favor of dredging the harbor. Both will also be against (although not very strongly) dredging other harbors. When they get into the House, the explicit bargaining scheme which is stable will explain their behavior. Unfortunately, there are many types of logrolling which take place at the platform level, hence the instability problem still remains.

Why do we not see this kind of change in the real world? One possible solution is simply that without the high degree of symmetry which I have imposed upon my model there may be genuinely superior coalitions. Riker discussed one particular set of conditions under which certain coalitions are "better" than others.[15] There may be many other similar situations.

This solution, however, obviously has its drawbacks and I think we can construct another solution which is both simpler and closer to the real world. In his recent article, Arrow pointed out that "Since the effect of any individual vote is so very small, it does not pay a voter to acquire information unless his stake in the issue is enormously greater than the cost of the information." These theoretical considerations which indicate that people should not bother to become informed about politics can be matched with empirical data which seems to indicate that they do not, in fact, know much about politics. If we assume that individuals will only make an effort to find out about policies when the effect on them is greater than a certain amount, then the individual would normally know, at least, something about what we might call public interest issues, such as police and national defense and also something about those logrolling issues which particularly concern him, i.e., those upon which his feelings are intense. However, he would not know anything about those logrolling issues which did not greatly affect him.

All the inhabitants of Richmond would know about the James River dredging project but few of them would know about the dredging of the river to Tulsa, Oklahoma. Under these circumstances, a political party making up its platform would assume that different voters have somewhat different information positions. In the extreme, the voter in Richmond would respond to a political world in which he saw general issues and the dredging of the James. In this area of his information there will be no possibility of strict logrolling and hence both political parties would choose approximately the center of this issue space. With our assumptions of voter ignorance of other issues, this would involve dredging the James to the level of ten. With many voters in Richmond, the point chosen would be the median of *their* preferences. The party also assumes similar positions with respect to other electorates which have different fields of knowledge and preferences. The outcome would involve logrolling in a sense that the individual groups would be given special treatment but would depend upon the ignorance of the voter with respect to the logrolling "payments" to other parties. Whether voters actually *are* this ignorant is something which can be questioned. Certainly they are opposed to taxes in general, and are aware of the fact that other people's projects, in one way or another, contribute to the tax load. The empirical investigations which do show appalling voter ignorance have never been addressed to this specific problem. Further empirical research would appear to be called for.

7

The Social Costs of Reducing Social Cost

During much of my career as a sort-of economist I have been a specialist on social cost. During the first part of this career, I continuously told people (and muttered to myself) that there were vast profits to be made in our society by reducing a number of obvious social costs. In recent years I find myself warning people (and muttering to myself) that, quite commonly, action taken to reduce these social costs turns out to be worse than doing nothing. It is my personal experience, in changing from an advocate of expanded government to an opponent of specific government action, that prompted this discussion.

If the government engages in an unwise action, it does not indicate that without government action the situation would have been ideal. Indeed, it seems undeniable that very large profits are available to our society from carefully calculated government action in a wide variety of areas where there are large social costs. I perceive the problem to be simply that the government is apt to impose social costs rather than to eliminate them.

Since it is not possible to talk about everything at once. I propose to omit from this discussion certain serious problems which democratic action can raise. The first of these is the Arrow problem, which is the prospect that democracy actually produces random results due to problems of aggregating preferences. I shall assume throughout this discussion that the voting process produces an outcome which is, on the whole, in accord with majority preferences and that terrible mathematical problems associated with democracy do not exist.

Secondly, I shall assume that the bureaucratic problems discussed in Niskanen's *Bureaucracy and Representative Government* have somehow been solved or, perhaps, are not real.[1] Using a simple maximizing model of the bureaucrat and looking at the type of institutional structure we have in our federal government, Niskanen argues that the profits from establishing a government activity are apt to be entirely consumed in the expansion of the bureaucracy itself. Thus, in equilibrium, in the Niskanen model, the society would be indifferent to maintaining the bureaucracy at the size it reaches or abolishing it. The entire profit of eliminating some social costs would be eaten up in the cost of supporting additional bureaucrats. Niskanen's arguments for the frequency of this phenomenon are fairly powerful, but here I simply assume that it does not occur.

In 1949, I was in North China. The country was backward, as it had been for a long time, and as it is today; furthermore, it was also disturbed by civil war. Nevertheless, the doctors there maintained that their medical practice was better than that currently in use in the United States. Their argument was that various new drugs were not permitted for general use in the United States because these drugs had not yet been approved by the appropriate federal authorities, but they were widely available in China.

Let us temporarily assume that these Chinese physicians were completely correct in their evaluation of the situation. Here was a case in which the federal government of the United States was attempting to reduce certain private costs – the prospect that in purchasing a product for my own use, I might find that I had been misinformed about its effects. But this action was generating what we must concede was a social cost, specifically, a government rule that reduced the availability of certain medicines in the United States. The government was taking action which, in this case, created a social cost where none existed before.

Obviously, this particular effect has been greatly magnified by the recent expansion of government control in medicine. It is clear that people who live outside the United States have certain advantages over us. They are able to purchase newly developed drugs immediately, rather than waiting the nine months or more that it takes to get government approval for sale in the United States. Furthermore, the cost of obtaining approval for sale has surely led to a reduction in total research for new medicines.

Note that my discussion so far does not indicate that these provisions prohibiting the sale of new drugs until they have been tested to the satisfaction of the federal government are, on balance, causing additional deaths. New drugs are, indeed, dangerous, although it should be noted that we have better technical advice in the purchase of drugs than in the purchase of any other single commodity. Restricting general use of such drugs reduces unexpected patient reactions, and this may be more important than the rise in death rate and the retarding of medical research that come from wide usage of such drugs. My point here is simply that the individual cost that is reduced through this particular bit of government action is clearly offset by a social cost.

An even better example of this phenomenon is the development of automobiles so designed that passengers are less likely to be killed in accidents. Clearly, this reduces the private danger to the driver and his passengers while it increases the social danger, as the driver of such a car presumably uses fewer resources in attempting to avoid accidents. If we were interested in actually reducing the social cost of automobile accidents – their externality component – we would go exactly opposite to the direction being taken by Ralph Nader. We would require that every car be equipped with a dagger mounted in the hub of a steering wheel pointing toward the chest of the driver; this would surely be a good device for reducing the likelihood that the driver would be killed through someone else's fault in an automobile accident. In a less radical vein, lowering the speed limits and enforcing them very vigorously sharply reduces the social cost of accidents but at the cost of imposing private inconvenience on individuals. Thus, we inflict a private cost in the sense that we compel the individual to purchase safety devices which he would rather not purchase in order to reduce the possibility that he will be killed and, thereby, increase the likelihood that other people will be killed.

Note that I have not argued that either of these policies is, in and of itself, undesirable. It may be that probable death rates would be higher under a system in which any type of medicine could be freely prescribed by a physician than under a system in which most new medicines are not generally available before very thorough testing. Similarly, the laws which make it impossible to buy a new car without a number of life-protecting devices built into it may, indeed, reduce the overall death rate from automobile accidents. In each case, however, the result is to generate a social cost in a fairly pure form. No social cost is eliminated.

Let me, however, return to my basic subject, namely, the effects that may be expected from efforts to reduce cost in a democracy. A recent problem in the generation of atomic energy is a simple example. There have been a number of sensational public claims that the Atomic Energy Commission has set its limits for radiation emission much too high. As a result, the AEC, although denying a response to pressures, has sharply lowered these limits. The result is, by any criteria including simple minimization of radiation with no other cost considered, highly uneconomical. If the cost of meeting these new standards were put simply as a tax on the atomic energy generation industry, with the returns used to reduce exposures to medical X-rays, then radiation exposure for the average American would decrease greatly. Furthermore, although the data are meager, it appears likely that replacement of a fossil fuel generating plant by an atomic energy plant, under present technology, would reduce the effective national death rate because the current atomic plants produce fewer dangerous contaminants in the air than do the fossil plants.

In fact, of course, the data on which all of these decisions are made are extremely incomplete. It seems likely that the best use of funds in this area would be to finance a search for better data and to defer further decisions based on present data. Nevertheless, on the basis of the data now available, it appears that the Atomic Energy Commission was not only wrong, it was pathologically wrong; and it is clear that the decision was the result of what we may call democratic factors.

These examples are by no means unusual. Indeed, something like this is the norm in government attempts to reduce social cost. Why may such behavior be expected in a democracy? Let us begin by taking Pigou's well-known example of the smoking chimney, which has become traditional in discussions of social costs. Suppose we have a factory chimney that smokes, and living around it are a number of people who dry their washing on an outside line. These householders suffer loss from the soot that accumulates on their clothing, but they cannot, individually, enter into an agreement with the factory owner because of the free-rider problem. Each individual could reasonably suppose that any payment which he might make to the factory owner to reduce smoke emission would have only a trivial effect on the total amount of smoke which fell on his laundry. Thus, even though the damage suffered by the householders may be much greater than the benefit obtained by the factory owner, no private bargains will be made. This is, of course, a motive for the householders to organize and form a uniform bargaining coalition; but, obviously it is less costly and certainly easier for the individual householder to stay outside of this bargaining coalition and enjoy its profits without making any payment. Under the circumstances, nothing is done, and we turn, following the traditional line of reasoning, to governmental control.

Given the possibility of governmental intervention each individual votes on the issue of smoke emission, and since the government will use coercion to require all people to carry out whatever decision is made by its democratic processes, no individual has any motive to conceal his preferences in this voting procedure. Therefore, according to this traditional line of reasoning, one should anticipate that this problem would be handled better by a democracy than by free-market activity.

This line of reasoning is unexceptionable as far as it goes, but the problem of information is not considered. The decision as to how much the factory smoke should be restricted, or what particular method should be used to restrict it – for example, by a tax on smoke emission – is a technical problem, but not a terribly difficult one. Should the individual voter take the trouble to become informed on these matters? Traditional reasoning indicates clearly that the voters should not bother. Just as each householder would find that his individual benefits from a payment to the factory owner are very small, so any time spent on gathering information would mainly benefit other people.

Indeed, the case is much stronger. I have not specified any particular voting model for the government of this community, but if the number of citizens exceeds about 100, in almost any voting scheme several propositions would be true. If the individual improves his information and hence changes the criterion by which he would vote, the odds are great that this change would have no effect whatsoever on the outcome; or if it does, the effect would be extremely small. Under the circumstances, the benefits of improved information are practically nil, and the individual would probably not bother to seek it. Hence, the free-rider problem returns. In the market with externalities, the individual can be a free rider in the sense that he does not make payments. In governmental dealing with externalities, the individual can be a free rider in the sense that he acquires no information, and therefore, his decisions are uninformed.

I began this discussion with examples of restrictions on the purchase of medicine and automobiles without certain safety devices. These examples were selected with malice aforethought. In each case, the advocates of these plans have argued that individuals are not well enough informed to make sensible decisions. In the case of medicine, the individual characteristically first selects an expert advisor and then purchases the medicine on the advice of this expert. The only argument for restrictions is that the individual may injure himself because he is inadequately informed. Note, however, that it is the individual himself who bears the full cost of any such injury. Surely he would be motivated to acquire information for making this decision more strongly than he is motivated to acquire adequate information whether or not to have a seat belt in his car. It must be assumed that he is not motivated to acquire information as to how he should cast his vote or to write his congressman on a particular issue.

Now it might be thought that all of this is a matter of little importance. The individual presumably has some preferences about smoke, which he can simply express by voting, leaving to others the problem of how those decisions shall be implemented. However, this attributes to the government apparatus some intellectual capabilities which it does not have, but let us defer that matter for the moment. The present question is simply whether the individual knows his own preferences well enough to cast an informed vote.

I presume that most people object to industrial smoke. The issue confronting the voters in this small hypothetical community, however, is not whether they object to the smoke, but how strongly they feel this preference. How much are they willing to sacrifice to reduce smoke emission? Thus, the individual voter, if he were to cast an informed vote, would have to go through an elaborate mental process in which he determined how much he would be willing to pay for various reductions in smoke level. Most people are not accustomed to this kind of thinking, and, moreover, the gain to each voter from undertaking it is virtually nil. Once again, we suspect that voters would prefer not to engage in this type of thinking.

If the voter does undertake any such analysis, however, he is likely to look upon the problem as one of obtaining not an optimum allocation of resources, but a transfer of wealth from the factory owner to himself. Hence, he is not particularly motivated to reach the correct conclusion. The situation is one in which the voter has substantially no motive to examine his preference with any care, but if he does, he is likely to ask the wrong question.

In practice, of couse, there may be offsetting public goods. The reduction in the factory smoke by legislation may reduce the likelihood of new factories settling in the area, and lead to lower average wages. Here again, the individual is offsetting two different considerations, both of which are fairly complicated; there is no reason why he should devote any energy to reaching the correct conclusion.

Before going further with my analysis of democracy, I should like to deal briefly with an alternative theory of social cost elimination which I think is quite widely held, although it is not usually articulated. According to this theory, the people do not actually make basic decisions, either by direct voting or by voting for politicians who make the decisions in terms of their expected benefits. Instead, civil servants make the basic decisions. Further, these civil servants are not deeply influenced by political factors. Indeed, they are a quite unusual group of people. Instead of being primarily concerned with their own careers and only secondarily interested in such matters as the public interest, they are a wise and objective group of people. These paragons, then, reach the correct conclusions because they are wise and devoted to the public interest.

Such decisions are, of couse, superior to market decisions. It will be noted, however, that there is no evidence that civil servants are one whit different from the rest of us. One can always "solve" any government problem by assuming a person or group both devoted to the public interest and intelligent. For example, we could assume that all business people are devoted to the public interest, and hence would never generate externalities except when it is in the national interest to do so. In the real world, however, the central problem is to design institutions that produce general benefits, even though each person is primarily interested in his personal well-being rather than the public interest. If we do, indeed, find exceptional individuals like those described above, it would be sensible to discontinue democracy and simply put them in complete charge of the government. I doubt that we are going to find such paragons in the near future.

To return to my main theme. I believe I have demonstrated that the voters are characteristically ill-informed when voting on reducing social costs. Furthermore, their primary concern is with wealth transferred to themselves, rather than with social cost efficiency. Logically, this would mean that a democratic government would be inefficient in reducing social costs. What type of behavior could we expect in such a government?

First, individuals would make their decisions not through careful thought or study, but as a result of information which came to them casually. Fad and fashion would be of tremendous importance. No one can look at the real world without realizing that this prediction has been fulfilled.

Subsequently, we would anticipate that media personalities and other people in a position to influence the current intellectual fashions would be of great importance in determining action taken in any given area. This would mean that individuals in television broadcasting, journalism, and so on could find their personal power and position in society improved by the expansion of government activity. Hence, these people might well be in favor of greater government activity in this area.

It is also conceivable that private corporations would develop fairly elaborate procedures set up for the sole purpose of influencing the media and, consequently, public opinion. Thus we could predict the modern phenomenon of the corporate president selected because he is thought to be able to present a good image for the company rather than because he is efficient. Other factors also contribute to the selection of such people, so the existence of corporate presidents of this sort cannot be used as evidence for our hypothesis.

A government official whether a civil servant or a politician, would also favor further government programs for purely selfish reasons. Washington, DC has recently blossomed forth with a number of very expensive restaurants, in which a single meal may cost $50. It is clear that these restaurants are not supported by the native rich of Washington, because there are none, nor are they supported by civil servants and congressmen, few of whom can afford such a bill. Who, then, does support them? A vice president of General Dynamics – who happens to live in Washington and who has been named to his position not because he is an engineer, but because he knows eight congressmen and 27 civil servants – is the characteristic customer. Further, these specialists on government manipulation do not, in general, take each other to lunch at these restaurants. The people they take to lunch are newspapermen, TV reporters, civil servants, etc.

Although I believe most American high-ranking civil servants are still unbribable in cash, they do find their living standards increased somewhat owing to their positions. Under the circumstances, it is easy to see why civil servants should be interested in expanding the power of the government to regulate (although they also have other good reasons for this particular bias). Also, it is fairly certain that major corporations are not wasting money when they establish Washington offices; they do indeed influence government policy in their own interests.

Thus, we could expect that the voters' lack of information and thought would lead both to an increased importance of fashion and other fluctuating influences, and to the manipulation of the system by various interest groups. Probably civil servants and the media are the most powerful special interest groups.

In order to discuss another characteristic resulting from lack of voter information, let me go back to one of the problems which was fashionable among intellectuals before ecology became the all-encompassing rage: fluoridation of water. Normally, if the question of whether water should be fluoridated was put to the voters, anti-fluoridation organizations staged a campaign and won. After a good deal of name-calling, some serious research was undertaken and an explanation for the vote was discovered. The pro-fluoridation people argued that a child who drinks fluoridated water throughout his childhood will have fewer cavities in his teeth than one who does not. In general, the reduction of cavities was proportional to the length of time the child drank the water; hence, delaying introduction of fluoridation by two or three years would result in only a fairly small change in what is, after all, a fairly small health problem for most children. The anti-fluoridation people, on the other hand, had much more spectacular changes, alleging, for example, that fluoridation caused cancer. Both sides produced technical specialists to argue their points, and the average voter was not able to choose between the competing technical experts.

The cost of delaying fluoridation was, even by the claims of its advocates, not very great. The cost of introducing fluoridation, on the other hand, according to the claims of its opponents, could be very great indeed. Under these circumstances, the voter chose to play safe.

We have observed the same behavior in a number of social cost problems in the United States. On one side is the utility president who argues that unless he is permitted to begin construction of a new generating plant within three years there will be power shortages at certain times of the year. On the other side are people who maintain that construction of the utility plant will cause fairly spectacular and serious damage. The voter is unable to determine the relative expertise of the specialists on each side and, hence, chooses to play safe by voting against the construction. We can hardly blame the voter for this conclusion, assuming that he has no motive to become informed and that (particularly in this case) becoming well informed would be quite difficult. Decisions of this sort lead to optimum allocation of resources only by accident. However, a large number of such decisions are being made today, and it is likely that the cost to our society will be quite great.

I must say, in this case, I do not have very much to offer as a solution. It is certainly true that social costs exist and are important and that the market in general will not deal with them adequately. The problem is that the government also deals with them badly. In essence, the market has a systematic bias toward producing certain kinds of "bads," and while the government has no such calculable bias, it does have a systematic tendency to take ill-judged action.

Under the circumstances, there is one very obvious recommendation. Government action should be resorted to only when the social cost emanating from the market is quite great. The level of efficiency of government action is apt to be low, and the possibility of damage through erratic, ill-informed decisions is great. The situation is like that of a person who was ill in 1700 and considering whether or not to call the doctor. The best rule was to call the doctor only if the person was *very* ill. The doctor, using the medical technology of the day, clearly brought with him a real chance of death from his treatment. Unless the possibility of death from the disease itself was greater, one was best advised not to call the doctor.

I have another recommendation which should occur almost immediately to any scholar, but, so far as I know, has not been proposed by anyone else. We should try to invent a new form of government. Democracy is at least 2,500 years old and probably older. It was developed by a group of very primitive people and was not the result of a great deal of careful thought. In general, with the advance of science we anticipate that we will be able to replace old devices and institutions with new inventions. One would therefore assume that a great many people are searching for a better form of government than democracy. This assumption is directly contrary to fact.

As far as I know, the strongest argument for democracy is Winston Churchill's statement "democracy is the worst of all possible forms of government, except those others that have been tried out from time to time." No one really regards democracy as highly efficient; the fact that it is better than despotism or consulting the augurs is surely extremely modest praise. I think we should begin an effort to invent something better. I myself have been trying to think of a better form of government for some time, and I must confess that I have failed totally. This does not mean that it is impossible. Democracy is not a holy institution, but a mechanism for achieving some fairly prosaic goals. It does not appear to be a very efficient mechanism. Under the circumstances, I can think of few more important fields for research than looking for something better.

8

Why So Much Stability?

One of Duncan Black's more important contributions was a classically simple proof that with complex issues and majority voting a stable outcome is unlikely.[1] This very simple proof that there would normally be no motion which can get a majority against all others, and hence that any possible outcome is dominated by another has been elaborated and made more precise by later work. Without most improbable conditions endless cycling would be expected. This is particularly true when logrolling is present as it normally is.

If we look at the real world, however, we observe not only is there no endless cycling, but acts are passed with reasonable dispatch and then remain unchanged for very long periods of time. Thus, theory and reality seem to be not only out of contact, but actually in sharp conflict. It is the purpose of this article to demonstrate that our existing theory when properly looked at, does indeed imply a relatively stable outcome to voting. In some cases, however, this stability will not be a true equilibrium because a random member of a large set will be chosen and then that random outcome will be left unchanged for long periods of time. It does not dominate all other outcomes, but is retained merely because of its particular history.

There are already several possible explanations for the observed stability in the literature. We will take them up as they become relevant to the general line of reasoning. I should, however, warn the reader that my own previous work, including joint work with Buchanan, will play a major role here. This may simply reflect egotism, but I think that some of the early work which is now partially forgotten can provide solutions for modern problems.

Much recent Public Choice work has involved spatial models and these models frequently ignore logrolling. The reason, presumably, is that it is very hard to put logrolling in a two-dimensional diagram. We shall begin considering such special models and assume that the issues are the sort that does not lead to logrolling, and then turn to more complex logrolling problems.

With respect to the first situation in which logrolling does not occur, there is already one possible explanation for the observed stability in the literature, my own "General Irrelevance of the General Impossibility Theorem".[2] I there argued that endless cycling is theoretically possible, but unlikely in practice if the number of voters is large. In oral discussion with various people, I have heard that my proof is not regarded as very reliable any more because McKelvey has proved that majority voting can reach any part of the issue space.[3] I can not regard this as a disproof of my argument. After all, I said "we should note that it is at least theoretically possible for the majority voting process to get outside the Pareto optimal area."[4]

To somewhat modernize the conclusions of my argument in the "General Irrelevance of the General Impossibility Theorem,"[5] if there is someone with strict control of the agenda and perfect knowledge of everyone else's preferences, and all people always vote their preferences, i.e., the agenda controller is the only strategist among the group, then the agenda controller can achieve his optimum regardless of where it is.[6]

If there are many voters then, unless the agenda controller's personal preference is near the middle of the cloud of optima in the issue space, his maneuvers will be readily detectable by simply examining the record. There will be a very long series of votes in each one of which the outcome is very close. As a general rule, one cannot move away from the general area at the center of the cloud of issue points except by tiny steps in which the majority is also tiny.

If there is no person in control of the agenda, i.e., we are following Robert's Rules of Order in its pure form, or some other procedure which permits anyone who wishes to make a motion, the procedure will move into the center of the cloud of issue points fairly quickly. The exact point at which it will come to rest is indeterminate because within the center endless cycling is possible. If we simply assume that small moves are ruled out, the process will in fact terminate, not because there are no other points that dominate the terminating point, but because all the points that dominate it are so close that they are not permitted to be voted on.[7]

There is another mechanism which can, of course, lead to the middle of the cloud of optimal points in this kind of a system, namely two-party voting. If there are two parties, both will choose policies near the center of distribution, hence the outcome, regardless of which party wins, will be near the center.

The above seems to me fairly simple and straightforward and also not terribly important, hence I have given it a rather brief treatment. The empirically important problem is the case in which logrolling is possible. Most government actions have the characteristic of giving a rather intense benefit to a small group at a small cost to each member of a large group. Simple majority voting would seem to indicate that such bills cannot be passed, but if several small groups get together and logroll they can. Unfortunately, this is very difficult to present in a simple two-dimensional diagram and we need algebra.

Table 8.1 shows a situation where a five member legislature, each member of which [A, B, C, D, and E] has a project which will benefit his district but injure all of the others. A, for example, would like Project A to be implemented at a level of ten and the others at a level of 0. The equations are loss equations, i.e. they demonstrate the injuries one will suffer at any point other than his optimum as compared to the optimum. The indifference hyper-surfaces are, in essence, five-dimensional ellipsoids shortened in one dimension, with each center at ten units on the axis favored by that member.

TABLE 8.1[8]

$$L_A^2 = 5(A - 10)^2 + B^2 + C^2 + D^2 + E$$
$$L_B^2 = A^2 + 5(B^2 - 10)^2 + C^2 + D^2 + E^2$$
$$L_C^2 = A^2 + B^2 + 5(C - 10)^2 + D^2 + E^2$$
$$L_D^2 = A^2 + B^2 + C^2 + 5(D - 10)^2 + E^2$$
$$L_E^2 = A^2 + B^2 + C^2 + D^2 + 5(E - 10)^2$$

With this particular mathematical representation, unanimous consent can be obtained for a joint project in which all five of the projects are implemented to some rather small amount. This is probably unrealistic if we are thinking of such logrolling activities as rivers and harbors legislation. But if we look at the government as a whole it seems reasonable that this would be so.

Note that it is by no means necessary that a project have a positive payoff as projects of table 8.1 do. One can imagine a situation in which the individual congressman will be led into very severely damaging his constituents. In figure 8.1, we have a 25 member legislature which is considering a set of 25 bills, each one of which will give $15 to a given constituency, at a cost of $25 in the form of $1 tax on each of the 25 constituencies. The individual congressman can decide either to join in the logrolling or refuse to do so. Figure 8.1 shows the situation which he would face granted that various numbers from one to 24 of his fellow congressmen are

	Don't logroll	Logroll
1	0	0
2	0	0
3	0	0
4	0	0
5	0	0
6	0	0
7	0	0
8	0	0
9	0	0
9	0	0
10	0	0
11	0	0
12	0	2
13	−13	1
14	−14	0
15	−15	−1
16	−16	−2
17	−17	−3
18	−18	−4
19	−19	−5
20	−20	−6
21	−21	−7
22	−22	−8
23	−23	−9
24	−24	−10

Each bill will pay $15 to a given constituency at cost of $25 in the form of $1 tax on each constituency.

Figure 8.1

engaged in logrolling. It will be observed that if only a few members of the legislature are willing to logroll, it makes no difference which policy he undertakes. If, however, 12 or more of his fellow congressmen are willing to logroll he is always better off if he logrolls than if he does not. This is true even though the ultimate outcome if everybody logrolls is a loss of $10 per constituency.

In Table 8.1 the injury inflicted on each member of the group from doing nothing is 22.2.[9] The injury inflicted if they engaged in the optimal quantity of the projects is 15. Obviously, they should, if they could reach agreement, adopt the optimal production. A simple majority of voting legislature, however, would be unlikely to meet that goal. Logrolling is called for.

Following *The Calculus of Consent* and my own *Entrepreneurial Politics*, there are two forms that logrolling can take – formal coalitions and individual bargains.[10] In formal coalitions, three of the members get together and form a "platform" which calls for production of seven and one-seventh units for A, B, and C, and 0 for D and E. This gives a loss of 12 to the members of the winning coalition and a loss of 25.6 to the two representatives who are not members. *Ex ante* individuals would not know whether they were going to be members or not of the coalition, and hence we can calculate an *ex ante* value which gives a weighting of three-fifths to the 12 and two-fifths to 25.6. This value is 17.4.

The other logrolling technique, and the one to which *The Calculus of Consent* was primarily devoted, involves individual bargains. Thus, Mr A makes a bargain with Mr B and Mr C under which they both agree to vote for his project and he agrees to vote for theirs. Mr B then, now having two votes – his own and Mr A's, makes a bargain with D under which Mr B's project is passed. Mr C, who also has two votes already, A's and his own, makes a bargain with Mr E and gets his project passed. Mr D and Mr E then close the circle, with the result that all five projects are implemented. In this particular case, the loss function for all is 17.2 which is slightly better than the *ex ante* payoff under implicit logrolling. A discussion of the general conditions under which one or the other form of logrolling would give the best results, by Geoffrey Brennan, is attached as an appendix.

Let us begin our discussion with individual bargain logrolling and then go on to formal coalitions. Firstly, individual bargains are likely to involve everyone, as in this case, because any individual who is being left out of the bargains can always offer lower prices for his vote and hence get back in. There is likely to be an equilibrium price for votes although in the real world things would not be as symmetrical as in our simple example. The outcome will not be Pareto optimal and the exact outcome is to some extent path dependent, but basically something rather similar to our seven and one-seventh all around will come out. This is a stable equilibrium but unfortunately a pretty inferior equilibrium. Too many of these projects are being provided by the voting system. It may, of course, as it is in this case, be better than nothing at all but still we would like to do something better if there were some way of doing so. In *The Calculus of Consent*, Prof. Buchanan and I implicitly recommended raising the majority, which improves the structure of the equilibrium but also makes it harder to reach. Currently, I would probably recommend the demand revealing process.[11]

So far we seem to have had no difficulty at all in explaining stability. In fact, all of our models have been more or less stable. The real problem in explaining stability, however, comes when we turn to formal coalitions. Although *ex ante*, the congressman would presumably be more or less indifferent between individual bargains and a formal coalition, it is always true that for the members of the majority coalition a formal coalition dominates the individual bargaining form of logrolling. Thus, if A, B, and C can form a permanent coalition among themselves they will be better off than they would be in a system of individual bargaining. Of course, this is paid for by D and E who are worse off.

The problem here is that this coalition is unstable. D and E can offer C a coalition in which he gets eight and they each take six. He will then have 9.6 which is better than under the previous coalition, and D and E will have 13.4 which is also an improvement. But this new coalition is similarly dominated by, let us say, returning to the original distribution for A and B, but leaving C out and substituting either D or E. The cycle is endless. The problem has been the subject of a great many quite sophisticated mathematical analyses but perhaps the simplest explanation is found in *The Calculus of Consent*.[12] The discussion there assumes a constant sum game. What we have here, of course, is a variable of sum game, but the variation, if anything, strengthens the argument.

There is a possible situation to this cycle, first suggested by von Neumann and Morgenstern and then elaborated in *The Calculus of Consent*.[13] Essentially, this explanation assumes that individuals would not like to be in the situation of C in the above second coalition because he realized that his payoff, which is much higher than that of the other members of the coalition, puts him in a particularly dangerous position in further negotiations. It is quite likely that A and B can buy off either D or E. Further, the cost to A and B would, in this case, be substantially nil since they would be in the same situation they were before C defected.

We can divide coalitions into two categories which we shall call egalitarian and aristocratic. Individuals who are members of an egalitarian coalition would be reluctant to join an aristocratic coalition. They would be reluctant for two reasons. One reason is that the serfs in the aristocratic coalition do not make as much as members of the egalitarian coalition. If they are offered the position of an aristocrat, however, they will fear that the coalition is radically unstable and that they are going to lose in the next round. If this suggestion of Neumann and Morgenstern is correct then egalitarian coalitions would be quite stable. We could not predict in advance which of the innumerable egalitarian coalitions would be formed, but we could predict that one would come into existence if logrolling with formal coalitions were the rule.

It should perhaps here be said that for both types of logrolling, the individual participants are well advised to sell out permanently rather than simply renting their vote. If they make a practice of voting for some project and then after they have been paid off voting for its repeal, they will shortly find that their vote is valued at very little by potential partners. Thus, we would anticipate logrolling bargains would tend to be fairly stable with respect to the particular things that were in fact voted through. They would not necessarily be stable with respect to future bills.

Note that once again, assuming that there is implicit logrolling and that the particular solution to the permanent cycle discussed above is correct, we reach a situation which is rather spectacularly non-Pareto optimal.[14] We do not know which particular coalition would form, but we do know that there will be overinvestment in projects of the members of the coalition and underinvestment in the projects of the minority.

So far then, we find that logrolling leads to two situations which are stable (in the sense of being unlikely to change) but non-Pareto optimal. Note, however, that the fact that these solutions are non-Pareto optimal does not mean that the world is not better off than it would be without logrolling. Indeed, in this particular example, the *ex ante* value of either kind of logrolling is greater than the *ex ante* value of prohibition of logrolling. We have here illustrated the general stand of *The Calculus of Consent* with respect to logrolling.

So far I have said nothing about the information conditions. There has been a sort of implicit assumption that everybody is perfectly informed. In the real world, of course, this is far from true, but, in general, the information conditions we expect of the real world will, if anything, reinforce all of our conclusions.[15] I propose to continue with what we may refer to as a more or less perfect information assumption throughout the rest of this article, not because I think it is true but because introduction of realistic information restrictions would lengthen this article without really improving it.

It has been pointed out by innumerable mathematicians that formal coalitions, from the standpoint of the members of the winning coalition, clearly dominates logrolling with individual bargaining. If we look at the real world, however, we find no apparent examples of this kind of logrolling. Let us confine ourselves to the American situation. I will discuss only the Congress of the United States, but I think most people will agree that the state legislatures – and for that matter city councils – will follow much the same pattern. The first thing we see is that almost everybody gets their share, i.e., congressional boodle is passed around more or less equally. That this is so is surely the conventional wisdom among political scientists, but there are, in addition, at least some reasonably formal demonstrations of the point. Butler looked at expenditures by congressional districts and in a quite sophisticated study and was unable to find any evidence of discrimination against any individual or class.[16] It is, of course, true that he was not able to totally rule out such discriminations, particularly since expenditures are only one of many variables which congressmen would regard as of value, but he tried all of the more reasonable patterns and found no result. Bennett and Mayberry found roughly the same situation, with benefits and taxes being distributed more or less in accordance with the number of congressmen and senators by states.[17]

It should be said that there is at least some empirical evidence which, it might be argued, cuts the other way. Beginning with Charles Plott, a number of scholars found that allocations and other benefits under the control of a given committee tend to be distributed disproportionately among the districts of the members of that committee and that the chairman, in particular, may do very well.[18] This is not inconsistent with the findings of Butler, Bennett and Mayberry, however. Since all congressmen are on committees, there is every reason to believe that this distortion by committee cancels out.[19]

Nevertheless, it cannot be said that exact equality is maintained, only that there are no groups who seem to be very decidedly left out. So far as I know, the only cases in which we have had groups literally left out occurred in the American South in two periods, the first period during the late Reconstruction when the Republican party was being exterminated by various state Democratic parties and in which the small Republican minorities in the legislature were given nothing, with the result that they tended to become smaller after the next election. The second case, also in the South, concerns the recent revival of the Republicans in that area. For a period, Democratic majorities in the legislatures once again prevented the tiny Republican minorities from getting anything. As the minorities became a little less tiny they were, however, admitted to the club. These are special cases; note that the dominant group in this case was not a mere 51 percent but usually something like 90 percent of the legislature. What happened was that individual bargaining logrolling proceeded but with a small group of people cut out. The implicit logrolling model was not adopted.

This tendency of the legislature to spread the benefits around throughout its entire membership has, generally speaking, not aroused much interest in traditional political scientists, probably because they do not know enough game theory to realize that it is, at least theoretically, unlikely. There are two basic explanations. The first, by Klingaman, points out that most people are risk averse and hence an even division of the spoils, which is less risky, might dominate a formal coalition.[20] The second explanation, which has been proposed by a number of political scientists, was put in its clearest form by Ferejohn[21]. It says rather little about risk aversion but argues the existence of a sort of ethic of universalism which leads everyone to feel that everyone else should get his share.

It will be noted that both of the above suggestions would point in the direction not of explicit logrolling, but of some kind of essentially Pareto optimal structure. It might, of course, be politically impossible to get a Pareto optimal scheme, but if the various members of Congress are actually interested, consciously, in a universal solution, surely they would not choose the inferior universal solution which comes out of logrolling with individual bargaining.

Here we have to turn to more general evidence, but I think no one who is even remotely familiar with the American Congress or other legislative bodies will doubt that what goes on is individual bargaining logrolling although, as I shall point out below, in some cases this leads to passage of portfolio bills which receive very nearly unanimous consent. Deals are made, however, and bills produced are very hard to explain in terms of cost–benefit ratios for the country as a whole, although they are frequently beneficial for the particular constituency involved. This does not, of course, mean that the constituency benefits from the entire collection of bills in the logrolling package but only from the individual one that affects the constituency. It loses on the others.[22]

Why are the formal logrolling coalitions so rare? Assuming that all of the coalitions will be roughly egalitarian in shape,[23] it is obvious that there are a great many possible coalitions, any one of which could have a majority. In general, however, none of these coalitions which equally divide the spoils among varying 51 percent combinations of voters, dominates the others. That being so, if such a coalition can be successfully put together, it will hold.

What then is the process of building such coalitions? Suppose that the entrepreneurs begin building competing proto-coalitions. The individual member of this collective group would be interested in both his payoff, if the coalition which he is contemplating at the moment is successful, and the probability of its success. This would lead to a complex bargaining procedure, but in this bargaining it will always be true that any coalition which looks like it has a good prospect of winning will immediately be attractive to further potential entrants, because the product of their payoff and the probability of success would rise with the probability that the proto-coalition would become a simple majority. This situation is rather similar to that at presidential nominating conventions as discussed by Brams and Riker.[24]

One would anticipate a slow bargaining procedure in which various individuals surveyed different proto-coalitions and then as it became clear that only a few or eventually only one had a chance to win, there would be a rush of people to join. The organizers of the coalition would, of course, not need more than 51 percent and hence would pay nothing for anybody who joined after they had achieved 51 percent, but it would be risky on their part to cut back on payments for the last few people needed for the 51 percent because of the prospect that this would lead to the very quick formation of a counter-coalition.

The individual, in bargaining to enter these coalitions, would face a tricky strategic problem together with, probably, the necessity of making decisions with information which is far from complete. He would know his potential payoff from entering the various proto-coalitions, but his information as to which one was actually going to win would not be very accurate during the period in which it would be of greatest value to him. Under the circumstances the outcome might well be quite random. We would anticipate that egalitarian coalitions would be formed, but we would not be able to tell in advance which egalitarian coalition would attain a winning majority.

Consider then, a continuing body which will, let us say, meet every year to deal with a bundle of governmental issues, with the bundle being at least to some extent different each year. Under these circumstances what kind of situation would we expect? Leaving aside the possibility of an agreed equal division among all, there are two clear-cut possibilities although we might expect various intermediate combinations in the real world. The first of these possibilities is that a single coalition would be formed at the beginning, again an egalitarian coalition, and that it would remain permanently in existence. If this occurred, once again we could not predict in advance what the coalition would be, but we could predict it would be egalitarian.

The other possibility is that there would be no such coalition. The prospect for the third logical possibility, the formation of a new egalitarian coalition each time that the body meets for all measures to be brought up at that time, is, I think, substantially zero. There certainly are at least some gains to be made through bargains that extend from one meeting to the next.

In real world legislative assemblies, the membership is not constant from year to year. Members die, retire, and are beaten in elections. A coalition of 51 percent would have to have some arrangement for admitting new members at each session and this would be difficult, albeit not impossible because presumably at each election the number of seats which had changed would be larger than the difference between the previous winning coalition and the minority in the previous session. Of course, it would be possible to maintain the coalition at a size large enough, let us say 60 percent of the votes, that it would still have a majority after the ordinary election losses. This would be particularly easy because members of the coalition would be less likely to lose elections than its opponents in view of the fact that they would do a good job for their constituency.

It does appear, however, that the bargaining problem faced by such a long-term coalition would be extremely difficult and very likely impossible. Consider an individual member or a small clique in such a coalition. In both cases, assume that their defection would convert the majority coalition into a minority coalition. For this individual or clique, there is no great advantage in being a member of the existing coalition over switching over and becoming a member, presumably a favored member, of a new coalition composed of the former minority. If this is so, they would be in a position to bargain very hard with the entrepreneurs of the majority coalition for good treatment.

Of course they would not want to become the aristocrat in an aristocratic coalition, but as we have said above, in the real world perfect egalitarianism is not possible because of the complex bundles of different kinds of measures which are passed by Congress. All of these measures have differential payoffs at different districts and, therefore, by definition some members of the coalition do better than others. The desire to be among the group that does better would presumably be universal in the coalition. Thus, hard bargaining for mildly special positions could be expected.

As part of this bargaining, they would periodically have to make realistic threats of departing. The counter-threats on the part of the management of the coalition, of course, would be to let them go and replace them with other people from the minority. This again, if the bargaining is efficient, must be realistic. Thus, the management of the coalition should practically continuously be seen to be engaging in negotiations with nonmembers of the coalition in order to keep the members in line.

Of course, it would not be one clique, but practically all members of the winning coalition, including for that matter the entrepreneurs themselves. All of them would be continuously threatening to leave if they don't get better treatment. Since this is a permanent coalition and since it is clearly possible for the benefits of the coalition to switch in a way adverse to any given member, such maneuvering is more or less necessary.

This kind of bargaining, however, is in the long run unstable. It is rather like the bargaining that went on between China and Russia before 1958. Each year the two parties would enter negotiations for the various aids of an economic nature which the Russians were offering to China, together with the political reciprocation that China was giving. Each year both would threaten to break off negotiations unless the other side offered more, but each year at the end they would reach agreement.

In the following year, however, each party would realize that last year they had finally given in and fear that the other party would assume they were going to do it this time, so they would find it necessary to engage in even more strongly threatening behavior.[25] Thus, each year the threats and other maneuvers intended to indicate to the other party that a break-off was indeed likely were increased. Each year, however, the evidence available to each party that the other party doesn't really mean its threats increases. Thus, it becomes even more important to use stronger techniques next time. Eventually, some kind of mistake is apt to be made and an actual break occurs.

These, however, are two-party arrangements. With a multi-party bargaining inside the dominant coalition, together with the good terms that can be offered from outside the dominant coalition, it is likely that the break will come fairly early. The new winning coalition, of course, would be equally unstable. The end product is apt to be the individually bargained logrolling model, with each congressman making a series of individual bargains with others because bargaining problems of attempting to maintain coalitions for a long period of time are too great. In any event, that is what we see in American legislatures.

The situation that we sometimes observe in European legislatures and, in particular, in the English legislature since 1900, in which there is a majority party or a coalition made up of several parties and the membership of the parties is permanent from election to election, but different parties in the government after elections is not clear. If we look at the actual performance of this type of government, we do not find that they attempt to confine the boodle to districts of the MPs in the winning coalition. The constituencies that apparently do best are the marginal constituencies, with the highly loyal constituencies on either side not doing as well.[26] Why this is true is not clear. Indeed, R. H. Crossman in his memoirs several times discusses the allocation of various funds, specifically housing funds, in such a way that safe Labour districts will do particularly well. It would appear, however, there is not great shift in the geographical location of government expenditure when Labour is replaced by Conservative or vice versa. The same seems to be true with the various coalition governments on the Continent. Why this is so, I don't know, and I suggest that someone do research on the point.

Congressmen are busy men and find themselves in need of time-saving devices. One simple procedure is to have the relevant committee which will, of course, contain representatives from both parties, canvass the House and decide which particular rivers and harbors bills would, in fact, pass if implicit logrolling were used on votes on each individual bill. This collection of specific projects can then be put together in one very large bill and presented to Congress as a unit. This saves congressmen time, but it has certain bizarre effects.

The first thing to be said is that the overall bill is contrary to the interest of all constituencies in the United States. This is because it is simply a summation of all the bills that would be passed by explicit logrolling and the bills that are passed by explicit logrolling normally contain many in which the cost is around twice as great as the total benefit.[27] The congressmen nevertheless will vote for them simply because they know that most of these individual bills will get through anyway and it is quite possible that if this rivers and harbors appropriation is turned down, the press of time will mean that some will not go through and the congressmen who vote against the major general bill are particularly likely to have the projects in their districts among those that are lost when the session adjourns.[28]

But here, once again, we have an equilibrium rather than an unstable outcome. The result is the same as that under explicit logrolling. The only difference is that a time saving device is used.

Recently, an even more radical time-saving device has been introduced in the formula allocation of funds. There is always a good deal of debate as to the exact techniques of the formula, and apparently pocket calculators are carried onto the floor and quick calculations are made as to how each constituency does. Still, this is a way of distributing the spoils which is even less time-consuming than simply combining a whole set of special projects into one bill. Indeed, it saves the time of the committee as well as the time of the congressmen on the floor. Looked at from the standpoint of the individual congressman, it has the unfortunate characteristic that he must anticipate that in some of the bills he will do badly on the formula and well on the others. But the logrolling in this case tends to run across bills, and a congressman who is willing to accept a particular formula on, let us say the allocation of food-stamp money in return for another formula on the housing allocations, will still do reasonably well.

With respect to these formula grants, however, it is possible that the legislature is moving towards the situation which we described in connection with our first example in which each bill is passed by a majority and benefits that majority, but in which there are many other possible majorities with, of course, different details of the formula which could just as well have formed and passed their own bills. The result under such arrangements would depend on the kind of coalition building we described in our first model with the various members of Congress anxious to be part of the winning coalition but, in general, unwilling to accept disproportional bids to move from one coalition to another because they realize this jeopardizes their position. Further, once the vote has gone through, the individuals would want to maintain their reputation for keeping their word and hence would be unwilling to vote for repealing or modifying it for at least a number of years. In this case, we would anticipate that the outcome would be one of the various possible egalitarian coalitions winning and that this outcome, although essentially random within that category, would tend to be stable over time.

I began by raising the question why we see as much stability as we do. I believe I have provided a theoretical explanation although, of course, it may not be either the only explanation or one which will withstand empirical examination. But my suggestion is that the stable outcomes that are observed and sometimes selected by procedures with a substantial random component are generally inefficient. They represent equilibria because the conditions needed to produce motion from some initial or intermediate position appear to be more severe than has been generally assumed.

Appendix

The crucial difference between "implicit" and "explicit" logrolling in the Tullock formulation is that in the former case only a minimal majority receives special-benefit legislation in its favor, whereas in the latter case everyone does. Hence, whether losses are larger (or benefits smaller) in the implicit than in the explicit case depends on whether the special-benefit legislation has positive net social benefits or not. If it does, then extending that special-benefit legislation to a larger number of voters must increase total social benefit: explicit logrolling is to be preferred.

A simple diagrammatic example may help lucidate. Suppose there are $2k + 1$ identical voters, each of which desires some project of purely private value. The demand curve of each voter for project size is shown as

D_i in figure 8.A1. If each voter paid for his own project, the size would be q_0, where D_i cuts the marginal cost curve of increasing project size, MC. This would be optimal. With collective provision under majority rule and general uniform taxes, the individual will aim to join a majority coalition which provides $(k + 1)$ of the projects, at a marginal cost for each of $(k + 1)/(2k + 1) \cdot MC$. The resultant project size will be q_M, which is inefficiently large.

Under implicit logrolling there will only be one such coalition, and the number of projects undertaken will be $(k + 1)$. Under explicit logrolling, there will be $(2k + 1)$ majority vote-trades and $(2k + 1)$ projects undertaken. Whether we should have $(2k + 1)$ projects or only $(k + 1)$ depends on whether each project of size q_M has positive net benefits. Consider the expected net benefit for any individual under explicit logrolling: this is the total benefit to him of his own project of size q_M, minus his share of the total cost of providing $(2k + 1)$ such projects. If we approximate the first term by the area under the demand curve over the range from zero to q_M (i.e. $\int_0^{q_M} D_i(q)dq$), then in the explicit logrolling case expected net benefit is simply:

$$E(B_i)^E = \int_0^{q_M} D_i(q)dq - \frac{1}{2k + 1}(q_M \cdot MC)2k + 1 \quad (8.A1)$$

$$= \int_0^{q_M} D_i(q)dq - q_M \cdot MC \quad (8.A2)$$

In the implicit logrolling case, the expected net benefit is:

$$E(B_i)^I = P_M\left[\int_0^{q_M} D_i(q)dq - \frac{k + 1}{2k + 1}(q_M MC)\right] - $$
$$- P_N \cdot \frac{k + 1}{2k + 1}(q_N \cdot MC) \quad (8.A3)$$

where P_M is the probability of being in the majority, $(k + 1)/(2k + 1)$; P_N is the probability of being in the minority; and $(k + 1)/(2k + 1)$ $(q_M \cdot MC)$ is the cost to each individual of financing the $(k + 1)$ projects of majority members.

Hence:

$$E(B_i)^I = P_M\int_0^{q_M} D_i(q)dq - (P_M + P_N)\frac{k + 1}{2k + 1}(q_M \cdot MC) \quad (8.A4)$$

$$= \frac{k+1}{2k+1}\left[\int_0^{q_N} D_i(q)dq - q_M \cdot MC\right] \tag{8.A5}$$

(since $P_M + P_N = 1$)

so $E(B_i)^I = \dfrac{k+1}{2k+1} E(B_i)^E$ (8.A6)

Hence, if $E(B_i)^E > 0$, then $E(B_i)^E > E(B_i)^I$
But if $E(B_i)^E < 0$, then $E(B_i)^I > E(B_i)^E$.

Diagrammatically, if the area *ABC* in figure 8.1A1 exceeds the area *CLM*, then the project, pursued at scale q_M, has positive total benefits, and explicit logrolling is preferable. Clearly, this need not be the case. In that event, implicit logrolling is preferable.

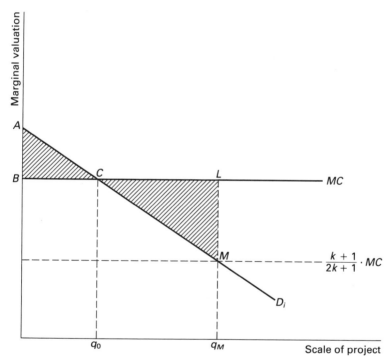

Figure 8.1A1

9

The Short Way with Dissenters

The problem of political terrorism is simply a modern version of a very old problem of dealing with people who commit political crimes (i.e, crimes motivated for political rather than economic gain). Today, and indeed traditionally (the pre-1917 Russian Communist Party, for example), these crimes sometimes involve getting money, but the money obtained from bank robberies or whatever it is, is, at least nominally, raised for political goals as well as individual benefit. As a matter of practical fact, the individuals who commit these crimes also live on the money they get, so there may be in this case some mixture of the two. Many of these crimes, however, will not bring in any funds at all to the people concerned; they involve killing someone or some kind of spectacular act which is intended to injure the government.

Note that when I refer to these as crimes, I am saying that they are crimes in terms of the existing law, but not necessarily that they are something that we should object to on other grounds. At the time the American Declaration of Independence was signed, Benjamin Franklin remarked, "We must now all hang together or most assuredly we shall all hang separately." This act which founded the present American government was, in fact, a crime under existing law. Thus, when I refer to terrorist acts as crimes, I am not alleging that they are any more wicked than General Washington besieging Boston, but merely that they violate the law. As a personal opinion, some of the modern terrorist groups are attacking very bad governments and others are attacking reasonably good governments. Myself, I would be reluctant to put somebody who is engaged in an effort to overthrow the present government of Mexico in the same category as somebody who is throwing bombs in present-day Italy.[1] But that is essentially a moral judgment. Let us now talk about this matter in positive terms and simply recognize that all of these things are indeed crimes, according to the domestic law, and the local government treats them much like other crimes.

It should be said here that, as a general rule, terrorism is not very prominent in really bad governments. Communist states and other efficient despotisms, whether the despotisms are the Nazis or something like the present government of Brazil have little or no difficulties. It is notable that the bulk of the immense fiction that has been produced about the underground opposition to Nazi Germany in World War II is indeed fiction. How Marshall Tito succeeded in convincing the West of the particular image he put out, I cannot imagine, but it may have something to do with the fact that the Chief of Staff of the British group that acted as his liaison was a member of the Communist Party.

If we look around the world, we find that terrorism is confined to two groups of states. First, democracies and second a group of rather inefficient despotisms. Some of the inefficient despotisms, in fact, are the creation of the terrorists. Uruguay and Argentina were more or less democratic states when terrorists began. They became dictatorships in reaction to terrorism. It is notable that only in Argentina, where the dictatorship has been weak and not very efficient, have they had great difficulty in putting down the terrorist activity.

But the purpose of this paper is not to judge the terrorists or their opponents, but to discuss the methods that can be used to suppress terrorism. I take it that most people will agree that what we might call being nice will not work. Democracy, rising living standards, civil liberties all seem to contribute to terrorism or, at any event, terrorism is more prominent in prosperous democratic states with active civil liberties than it is in the other kinds of state. Argentina is rapidly deteriorating, but it should not be forgotten that it used to be the most prosperous country in Latin America. That other formerly highly prosperous Latin American country, Batista's Cuba, has under Castro had substantially no difficulty with terrorism, even though it is one of the unusual countries where the living standard instead of rising is actually falling. Of course, they have neither democracy nor civil liberties there.

What then are the best methods of dealing with terrorism? The usual methods of dealing with any type of crime are the carrot and the stick. It is true that the normal discussion of dealing with crime emphasizes the stick, but the carrot, in fact, is part of all legal systems and probably should be emphasized more in the case of terrorism than most areas.

As far as the stick is concerned, most Western countries have confined themselves to three punishments: fines, imprisonment, and execution, and many of them have in fact abandoned the use of execution. The countries that really do very well against terrorism normally use torture of one sort or another as a punishment in addition to using it frequently in investigation. Russia, for example, has a set of rather nasty things that happen to their political criminals that don't happen to their ordinary criminals. I should say, however, that it does not seem to me that this type of torture of people who have been convicted is in any sense necessary or even particularly likely to reduce the degree of terrorism. The death penalty in itself should be adequate.

Those countries that have given up the death penalty have handicapped themselves in dealing with terrorism. The one exception to this is Israel and in Israel apparently a good many terrorists are in fact killed, although not after trial – it is always done before. If they are convicted, however, they are given very long sentences in prisons which are as unpleasant as the Russian prisons.

The basic problem with the use of imprisonment rather than the death penalty for dealing with political criminals[2] is not that it is not severe enough, but that criminals who believe that they are attempting to overthrow the existing government may not be particularly perturbed about a long prison sentence. They assume that the sentence will in fact be rather short because of the dawn of the red revolution and, as a matter of fact, the only result of getting put in prison is that they are protected from being shot at during the course of the revolution.

There is, of course, another characteristic of the long prison sentence which is that the revolutionary group may seize an airplane, embassy, etc., and threaten to kill large numbers of people unless some of their prisoners are let out. It is notable that even Israel has on one occasion released prisoners under these circumstances. To say that government should simiply refuse to do so is easy but one can be sympathetic with the government officials who decide that they will make the exchange. If they have no one on hand in their prisons because of prompt executions, the problem will never arise.

This argument for the death penalty in political crimes you will note has nothing to do with the feeling that they are particularly wicked. I would recommend it to the present government of Mexico, even though I regard the present government of Mexico as a pretty nasty organization, and would favor at least some of the groups that oppose it. I would also recommend it, although the recommendation is not strictly speaking necessary, to such governments as those of Argentina, South Africa, Israel, and the Soviet Union.

If you are going to use imprisonment as punishment for political criminals, however, you must have some idea as to what you will do if their colleagues seize hostages and demand their release. If you are able to break up the entire political organization simultaneously there is no problem here. The situation in this respect would be much easier if it were not that there are currently in the world many individual governments who are perfectly willing to give support to terrorist movements in other countries. This in general means that one cannot, strictly speaking, wipe out any terrorist group because a good part of it is abroad and its financial and armament resources come from abroad. Under the circumstances the death penalty seems to be called for.

The mention of the problem of hostages here, however, raises a number of major problems in any kind of dealing with political terrorism. In a way the situation is warlike, and if government can use sticks and rewards against the terrorists, the terrorists can do it against the government too. Thus, the terrorists may not only seize ordinary hostages, they may attempt to kill police or military officers whom they regard as particularly effective in dealing with the terrorists. Under these circumstances the police or military may become relatively ineffective because its members do not want themselves or their families to be killed.

This phenomenon can go further. In pre-World War I Russia, there was an active terrorist organization which apparently did not have very much information on which members of the police force were effective against it. It should be remembered that the highest ranking official of the Communist Party of Russia in Russia was in fact a police spy, but did have good information about who was engaging in political activity which was inconvenient to them. They thus killed people who criticized them in print. It seems likely that one of the results of this was a sharp change in publicly expressed political opinion in Russia. If you heavily attacked the left you might get killed and hence fairly few people did it. In a way the Black Hundreds were carrying out an effective censorship program.

But in any event, this particular type of activity in which the terrorist group attempts to use sticks against the government is one in which, if the government is sufficiently ruthless, the terrorists are almost certain to lose. It does indicate, however, that there is much to be said for keeping the names of the more active members of the government suppression force secret. This secrecy may have to be long-lasting. The Irish Republican Army, during the years after Ireland acquired independence, carried out a number of revenge movements against individual people whom they suspected of informing and who had been moved by the British government as far as Australia. We will return to this matter shortly when we talk about not government officials but witnesses for the prosecution.

But all of this assumes that the government has some idea of who the terrorists are. Traditionally, this information comes from three sources. The first of these is the sort of accidental development of information which is so important for any kind of police work. The criminal leaves physical evidence at the crime which makes it possible to identify him, he is seen by a casual passer-by who identifies him, or he is under investigation for some other reason and evidence of this particular crime turns up. This is important for all kinds of police activity, certainly important for dealing with terrorism but it does not involve anything very special.

The second source is, of course, the use of torture for suspects in order to get further information. Although Bentham himself said there were certain circumstances in which torture should be used and it is fairly easy for anybody to think up examples in which he personally would favor the use of torture, it does not seem to me that these situations are very common. In general, although there is, as I shall point out below, a good reason for the use of torture by inefficient governments dealing with terrorists, a reasonably efficient government will rarely, if ever, be confronted with one of these imaginary cases in which one might imagine torture to be desirable.

But assume that we do have a government which, like the Brazilian or the Argentinian or the Russian or, for that matter, the Chinese government, has decided to use torture for the extraction of information about terrorists. The first problem is that of whom to torture. No one is going to volunteer for this purpose and the end product is that you begin torturing people whom you, for one reason or another, suspect of being involved in the terrorist activities. More often than not this suspicion comes from their overt political activity. I would not want to deny that people who take a firmly left-wing position in Argentina or firmly right-wing position in Russia are more likely to be guilty of some kind of subversive activity than the population as a whole, but it should be kept in mind that this is only a probability not a certainty. Torturing individuals who have brought themselves to the attention of the authorities in this way is unlikely to be productive in most cases. A sufficiently ruthless government, of course, may be perfectly willing to do it for the purpose of getting the one person in ten who is actually guilty.

It should be emphasized by the way that torture should not be used for the purpose of extracting simply a confession. That's too easy and you'll get many innocent people. The point of the torture, if it is resorted to, should be to obtain some information which is independently confirmable and which indicates, first, whether or not the person you're torturing is guilty, and second, if possible, other members of his cell.

In general the first thing to aim for is positive confirmation of the guilt of the person concerned because under torture a perfectly innocent man may implicate other people who are also equally innocent. This may extend to a long chain of torturing innocent people which is not only nasty but also a waste of time and resources. As far as I can see most of the South American governments have fully understood this matter although it is arguable that the Russians have not. South American torture, if one gives credence to the accounts of people who have undergone it, is very unpleasant but it does not seem in general to be motivated simply by an effort to extract a confession of guilt. In general, they are looking for something more which is what they should do. Further, they do in the long run release people whom they come to conclude are innocent. Needless to say, they do not pay the extremely high damage claim which would be necessary to make the people whole from their torture.

For an efficient government, however, I believe that torture is something that seldom, if ever, need be resorted to. Many of the South American governments are not efficient and some socialistic governments, such as that of Russia, also may be driven to it. The reasons why it is suitable only for this kind of government will be dealt with later. Meanwhile, let me turn to what I regard as a superior method of getting information, which is simply offering large sums of money for it.

The first thing to be said about this method is that of course there is no need for the police or anyone else to seek out people who are possibly or probably guilty. All that is necessary is to announce these large sums and then wait quietly until people come to claim them. One of the problems with this system in the twentieth century as opposed to the nineteenth is that the amounts do not seem to be very large. The police apparently prefer to spend $50 or $60 million in police investigative time to catch a given criminal as opposed to offering one million dollars for that person. Why a police bureaucracy would feel this way is, of course, obvious but it is not so obvious why the government should permit police bureaucracies to maximize their size in this manner.

I am not at all clear in my mind why the amounts of money that are now being offered for information of this sort are so comparatively low. I once saw an advertisement in a German custom office which offered a total pyment of almost DM500,000 but it involved the detection of 18 separate people, with, of course, payments for each individual person. Five hundred thousand dollars a piece would have seemed to me more reasonable. Further, in this case, it was a collection of named people. An offer of, let us say, DM2 million for information leading to the arrest of any terrorists would no doubt have been more productive, since presumably the police do not know the names and do not have the pictures of all the terrorists.

There are a number of problems raised by use of large cash payments of this sort. Before turning to them let me digress briefly in order to explain why certain South American countries and perhaps socialist countries find it necessary to use torture instead of this method. In the South American countries the basic problem is corruption on the part of the police. If you provide large sums of money for detection of terrorists, one can assume that the police will try one way or another to deviate the money into their own pocket. Further, a potential informant would assume that he wasn't going to get very much of that money and hence would be less strongly motivated to produce the information. Under the circumstances the payoff of rewards is likely to be much less than in more efficient and honest governments.

The problem with socialist socities is not necessarily the dishonesty of the officials, although, of course, there is a good deal of that in socialist societies as well as non-socialist socieities, but the fact that they tend to be egalitarian. Under the circumstances they are unlikely to be willing to make individual citizens of their society very wealthy. They are particularly likely to feel that citizens of their society of low moral character should not be made very wealthy. Under the circumstances they are unlikely to be willing to offer large sums of money for information. Thus, they may be driven to torture as a replacement. In these cases it is likely that the government decision will be simply not to use large sums of money and the police will then be under pressure to produce results which may lead them to engage in torture, although possibly their government will be quite surprised about it. In the particular case of the Russians and Chinese, of course, that was not so. The government was fully informed of what was going on.

It should be said that the Russian government in particular sometimes has been quite ingenious in providing sizeable rewards for people who produce information. At one point they broke up rings in Easy Germany that were smuggling people to the West by the simple expedient of offering exit permits to the West for the person (together with his family) who gave them information on the organization of illegal departures. This reward, which was very nicely calculated to appeal to just exactly the people who would be best informed about such prospects, was quite successful.

But this was a special exception to the usual socialist rule. Let us assume we are dealing with a Western government that has no particular objection to making its citizens wealthy. Even so there are a number of difficulties raised by payment for information. The first of these, and an obvious one, is that people have a motive to produce fake information. This is a problem which police are fully accustomed to in almost all areas although large rewards, of course, make it worse. There is a straightforward solution: simply insist that collaborative evidence be available. Thus, if someone comes into the office and says that he knows the name of a terrorist, the police should insist that the reward will only be paid if, when they arrest the suspected terrorist, they find evidence indicating that the suspicion is correct.

This is an elementary precaution and in general raises no great difficulty although the prospect that the police will occasionally be fooled or that in some cases genuine information will be disbelieved because the terrorist has been careful enough to cover his traces is real. If, however, the police are normally right in this activity, and there is no reason they shouldn't be right much more than half of the time, they should be able to wipe out the terrorist if enough people report to them. The latter is partly a matter of the size of the rewards, a matter completely under the control of the government, and partly of problems having to do with the organization of the terrorists.

Let us now turn to the defenses of the terrorists themselves against this kind of informer. The first and obvious one is to threaten the life of the informer. The answer to this from the standpoint of the police is equally obvious, that is, to try and keep him hidden. Since the time of President Kennedy we have had in the United States a witness anonymity program, actually invented not by President Kennedy but by his brother, Robert, who was at the time Attorney General. Under this program people who have testified against criminals who might seriously jeopardize their lives are provided with new identities. The program has not worked very well, essentially because it is primarily dealing with common criminals and apparently the police officials who administer it dislike their charges. Nevertheless, there is no reason to be particularly dubious as to the possibility of working such a program efficiently.

This is particularly true, I should say, if you happen to be in either an English- or Spanish-speaking country.[3] With these languages so widely spoken around the world it is fairly easy to move someone to a totally different country where nevertheless he continues speaking his native language. An American would not be terribly disturbed on being moved from Chicago to Sydney, Australia nor would an Australian be deeply disturbed on being moved from Sydney, Australia to Chicago. With suitable faked papers there is no reason for this not to be completely successful.

The other procedure here, of course, is simply to destroy the terrorists' group so that there is no one remaining who is likely to try and take revenge on the person who broke the group up. This may be difficult but it is certainly not impossible, and there have been many cases in which it has successfully been done. Those who have read the Sherlock Holmes story *The Valley of Fear* know that, in fiction, a group which was destroyed by detectives in the United States, tracked down their destroyer and killed him in England. In actual fact, however, the Molly MacGuires, whose destruction provided Conan Doyle with the idea for this story, were destroyed and the Pinkerton men responsible for it lived long and reasonably productive lives without any fear that they would be attacked by the people whose group they had broken up. The total destruction of such a terrorist group, in at least the first few moves, is, however, unlikely and hence some other method of providing protection should be looked into.

It should, of course, include not only the individual but his family. Recently the Italian government decided to purchase information by simply remitting part of the prison sentences of people who were willing to inform on their confederates. This is, of course, a fairly old idea and the remarkable aspect of the Italian program in this area was simply they were so modest at it. The reduction in sentences that they offered were really very slight compared to the importance of the information. In the United States a member of any criminal conspiracy who tells on other members of his group who have not yet been arrested can expect to be released without any charges at all. He can even take advantage of the anonymity program described above.

The Italian terrorists, however, in this case turned to attacks on the family of the informants. One very simple way to deal with this kind of problem which does not even involve protecting the informants' families, is simply to keep the identity of the informant a secret. This, if his evidence is to be used in court, is impossible in most Western countries, but it does not seem that there is any strong reason why the terrorist under trial must know the identity of the witnesses against him. We happen to have a particular system of trials to which we have become accustomed, but there is no strong evidence that it is a terribly desirable system.[4] The English, incidentally, have intriguing ways of getting around this problem. Prisoners of state, that is, those who are thought to be particularly likely to overthrow the government, are given a perfectly ordinary trial in the Tower of London, complete with defense attorney and confrontation of witnesses. If they are found guilty they are locked up in the Tower and kept incommunicado for the next ten or 12 years, with the result that they are not able to tell their confederates outside who the witnesses against them were and hence there is no way of taking revenge.

Other schemes of a similar nature, mainly a result of difficulties in Ireland, involve such matters as having a police officer simply testify that he has received information that so and so is a member of the IRA. This is regarded as adequate evidence for conviction under special acts of Parliament and, of course, it means that the informant is kept secret. Myself, I would much prefer that the judge or judges be given full access to the informants, even if the defendant is prevented from knowing who they are.[5]

It perhaps should be pointed out here, as a sort of digression, that there is substantially no difference between the use of torture to extract information and the use of a long sentence in prison to extract information. In other words, if you tell somebody that if he doesn't tell who his confederates are he will be tortured, it is not greatly different from telling him that if he doesn't tell who his confederates are he'll go to prison for 20 years. It is not obvious which one of these is the "more humane." We are accustomed to the remission of prison sentences as a way of getting information and not to torture, but we should try to avoid having our current customs enshrined in tables of gold. I, myself, as I've explained above, do not believe that torture is a suitable method simply because the payment of rewards almost always dominates it, but that does not mean that I feel that the use of remission of sentence is a markedly different techniques.

But one of the problems that I'm sure most people will raise at this point is the allegation that terrorist groups are not the types who will talk for monetary gain. It will be argued that they are fanatics and not subject to such mundane rewards. It is no doubt true that some people are more susceptible to monetary rewards than others, and it may perhaps be true that terrorists are less so than others. So far the use of large monetary rewards has not been tried, so we don't have any positive evidence on this. But there are reasons for believing that the reward system would work.

First, it should be pointed out that these fanatic terrorists don't seem very fanatic. If you take almost any estimate of the number of people who are members of, let us say, the Bader–Meinhoff gang, the PLO, or the IRA, and then divide this by the number of outrages they have perpetrated it can be seen that they aren't very busy in terrorist activities. One act of terror for every 10 man-years would seem to be not a bad average.

Further, if we look at the present-day terrorists they are frequently supported in considerable comfort by various foreign governments for one reason or another. In fact, in the 1960s they were frequently supported by reasonably wealthy members of their own community who happened to have left-wing sympathies. They made a fairly good thing out of their terrorist activities, and they put themselves in a situation in which it was hard for them to break away. The fact that they then only rather rarely chose to cooperate with the police doesn't prove that they would not have done so had they been provided with an easy way of doing it together with a promise that they would be wealthy for the rest of their lives if they did.

This is particularly likely since terrorist groups are like other human organizations in that various difficulties always arise within them. Jim Smith is mad because he had thought that he was going to be head of the local group and in fact Joe Jones got the job. Under the circumstances he may take his resentment out on Jones by seeing to it that Jones meets the public executioner. This is particularly likely if he is highly paid and protected if he informs. There may, and frequently are, sexual hangups in which one member of the group takes a girl away from another and that leads to a denunciation. The normal human frictions are likely to be magnified by the prospect of very great wealth if you break with the group. Further, just simply changing one's mind in politics does occur. Today it normally means that the person may try to drop out of terrorism which can be dangerous. If when he changed his mind he were promised a large sum of money and protection if he were to denounce the others, we would probably find far more denunciations.

Last, but by no means least here, there is the problem of new recruits. If a program for large rewards were known to exist, then one of the reasons for taking up left-wing politics in the university and gradually becoming a terrorist would be the fact that your uncle in Pittsburgh had told you that there was an opportunity to buy a McDonalds franchise for $500,000. There is no obvious way that the terrorists could tell recruits motivated in this manner from those who were genuinely politically motivated. Under the circumstances the terrorists themselves might establish security procedures which would paralyze them.

In sum then, I am proposing that we turn to the standard method of crime control, a mixture of the carrot and the stick for dealing with terrorism. Currently, the carrot is used hardly at all and when it is used, it is used simply in the form of somewhat lower prison sentences, while the stick is used in an inefficient way. Prison sentences are unpleasant, but to the terrorists they are less convincing than a death penalty would be. Note that my recommendations here are essentially nonpolitial. If we observe the world, we observe that a lot of nasty governments, such as the current government of North Korea or the former government in Uganda, have no problem with terrorists, because of the use of the carrot and the stick (frequently very inefficiently). A number of nice governments, on the other hand, such as those of West Germany and Italy, have a great deal of difficulty, because they don't make use of these techniques. It is clear that simply improving the political nature of the government will not cure terrorism, because the terrorists are commonest in those governments which seem to be politically best. Turning to other methods is therefore sensible.

In a way, I am proposing that the present situation be reversed. Currently, the terrorists use the death penalty against their enemies and offer quite substantial rewards for their friends. These substantial rewards, which come partly from various foreign governments and partly from bank robbery and kidnapping ransoms, are not particularly new in terrorist activity. Stalin, after all, organized a number of bank robberies to support the Communist Party of Russia. Further, one wealthy Russian who personally was a leftist provided funds for the Russian Community Party out of piety. Nevertheless, currently all these rewards to terrorists seem to be larger than normal. The police, in efforts to deal with the terrorists on the other hand, use very little in the way of the carrot and something, but not too much, in the way of the stick. I propose that the police take advantage of their superior resources to offer larger carrots and wield heavier sticks.

10

Income Testing and Politics: A Theoretical Model

Anyone examining the provision of income transfers or special services by the modern democratic state immediately realizes that a large amount of services are provided to people who are by no means poor.[1] The farm programs which in almost every democratic country exploit nonfarmers for the benefit of farmers tend to benefit these farmers in proportion to the amount of agricultural land they hold. The benefits are not confined, for example, to poor farmers. Perhaps the extreme case of a categorical aid program for a group that is not poor involves a very large bundle of services and special facilities provided by the American and indeed most other democratic governments for owners of private aircraft – surely one of our more prosperous groups. It would not be particularly surprising if the facilities provided for them by the government would make them among the largest per capita recipients of transfers. These programs, however, are not the subject matter of this paper and they are relevant only insofar as their mere existence indicates that motivations for transfer activities in a democracy are frequently simply the desire of the recipients to receive the transfers rather than any desire to help the poor.

There are two different kinds of income-tested program. In the first, the full service is provided below a certain income and above that point, none. Thus, for example, we might have programs under which everyone whose income is under some particular amount gets free medical attention from the state and anyone whose income is above that gets no such attention. The second could be termed a negative income tax where services are provided on a graduated scale. This sliding scale program would provide that at some fairly high income the state would assist in catastrophic illness cases and, as income fell, gradually add additional services until the very poor found even routine dentistry paid for.

Although administratively and in practical terms the decision of which of these two types of program should be selected is of great importance, I am not going to deal with that issue in this essay.

My line of reasoning will apply to both types of program. I will devote more discussion to the type in which there is a sharp income cutoff because it is analytically a little easier. I will, however, give enough attention to the gradual cutoff type so that the phenomena discussed in this chapter appear to be equally relevant.

In the countries in which universal services are provided – education in the United States, medicine in England, etc. – there is usually also a special privately provided supplementary service for the upper-income groups. The private schools in the United States and the approximately 5 percent of the population in England who carry health insurance in order to use the services of private doctors are examples. In Russia there is a government program to provide special medical facilities to upper-ranking members of the hierarchy.[2]

In this I will mainly ignore these supplements for upper-income groups for convenience of analysis. Our basic subject will be a comparison of income-tested and universal programs, using medical provisions as an example.

There are three different ways in which medical provision could be distributed. First, everyone would pay for his own. In practice, no doubt, this approach would be accompanied by a good deal of private charity. However, I will not discuss this, not because I think it is unimportant but because it complicates the analysis and is not vital to our subject. The second way of providing medical treatment is to have a tax-supported system which provides medical aid only to the poorest part of the population. In the third case the state provides full medical care for everyone. It could be assumed in both the second and third cases that the state-provided aid is (at least by intent) all of the medical services that the individual will receive.

A Political Model

Let us begin with a very simple political model. I should like to emphasize strongly that the consequences we draw from this political model are very heavily affected by the detailed assumptions about things such as preference curves and number of people. Thus, no direct transfer of the conclusions from the model into the real world is possible. The model has been designed, however, to be extremely simple and straightforward and hence easy to follow. As we work our way through the model, I will discuss the modifications that would be necessary to fit it to a more realistic set of assumptions about the real world.

We consider then a very simple society in which there are three citizens: Mr 1, who has an income of $100 a year; Mr 2, who has an income of $200; and Mr 3, who has an income of $300. At the beginning of our system there is no government-provided health care and Mr 1 is paying $5, Mr 2, $10, and Mr 3, $15 for medical care each year. Let us suppose, however, that Mr 2 and Mr 3 become concerned about Mr 1's welfare. They feel that more than $5 is needed to keep him in a reasonable state of health. They therefore propose a government program which will provide him with medical care at the expense of the taxpayer.[3]

Here we must make an assumption about the tax structure: i.e., taxes are proportional to income. That means for every dollar spent on Mr 1's health, Mr 1 will pay one-sixth of $1, Mr 2, one-third, and Mr 3, one-half. In figure 10.1, I show Mr 1's demand for medical care, and the demands by Mr 2 and Mr 3, not for medical care for themselves, but for medical care for Mr 1. The medical care cost is shown in constant value amounts by a horizontal line. Mr 1 would purchase the amount 0, which is equivalent to $5 in the private market. When we switch to government provision, however, prices change. Let us begin by considering what benefit level each of the three would favor for Mr 1 assuming that it be paid for by the taxpayer (i.e., by the three parties in proportion to their income). I have drawn in the cost to each per unit, and we observe that Mr 1's demand curve crosses his cost at point 1, Mr 2's at point 2 and Mr 3's at point 3. With the particular tax scheme that I have imposed on my model, this is a simple case of single-peaked preferences, and the median preference voter Mr 3 will prevail. Under this system Mr 1 will receive somewhat more medical care than before, perhaps $6 worth. He will also pay much less than before, about $1.

Before we go on to compare this outcome with what we would expect under universal medical care, let us take a closer look at these results. First, note that wealthy Mr 3 is median voter, not middle-class Mr 2. This is obviously an artifact of how the diagram was drawn, but it was done this way to emphasize that this condition can and indeed is not particularly unlikely to exist. Wealthy people presumably have a greater demand for charity as well as other things than people with less money. On the other hand, they normally pay a larger share of the taxes. Whether this will lead them to want more or fewer transfers to the poor then do the middle class depends essentially on the income elasticity of demand for charity. Nothing can be said about it *a priori*.

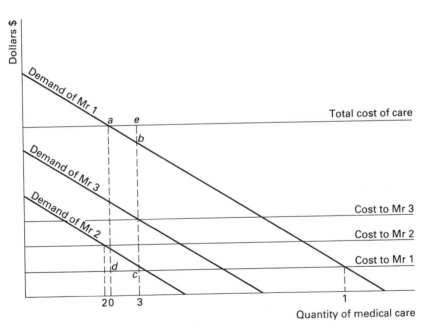

FIGURE 10.1 *Demand for medical care for poor voter (Mr 1) by Mr 1, by middle-income voter (Mr 2), and by rich voter (Mr 3) under income-tested provision of medical care.*

The second point we notice is that this outcome does not have a great deal to commend it in strict welfare terms. It is not the social optimum which would be obtained by summing the three men's curves and observing where that sum crosses the cost line and hence is not Pareto optimal. This is a general characteristic of direct-voting outcomes. Furthermore, it is not obvious that anybody except Mr 3 would be very happy with this particular outcome. Mr 2 finds himself being taxed to provide more medical attention for Mr 1 than he wants to give, and Mr 1 is, of course, receiving far less medical attention that he would like at that price.

Note also, and this is again a general characteristic of all government-provided programs for medicine, that although if given his choice Mr 1 would select the total quantity of medicine for himself shown by 1 on the horizontal axis when voting, if that amount has been provided, he will attempt to get from his doctor not that amount but the amount where his demand curve crosses the horizontal axis. As a voter he counts the cost of medical treatment to him as one-sixth its actual cost, as a consumer of a service on which there is no marginal charge at all, he counts it as 0.4 Hence he will try to repeat a very general characteristic of provision of "free" services. The voters *qua* voters take into account the cost, the voters *qua* customers of the free service do not, and hence we find the amount of service provided is always less than that which is "demanded." There must be some kind of rationing system, whether that would be waiting in long lines or arbitrary decisions by doctors.

It should also be noted that Mr 1 has another reason for being angry – he would prefer to receive the $6 in cash than in the form of medical attention. The recipient is better off if he is given cash and the principal beneficiaries from making it in-kind are either upper-income groups who suspect he would just drink it up or the actual providers of the service (doctors, etc.) or both.

Let us before we move to our next model note one final characteristic of figure 10.1. Mr 2 may well be still consuming more medical attention than Mr 1. To a considerable extent this reflects the fact that we have only three citizens in our model. Although I will not draw the diagram, consider the situation if we had not three but nine citizens and that the one at the bottom (the bottom 11 percent) was the only one who was regarded by the others as too poor to handle his own medical expenses. This would mean that the cost to each voter of providing medical services to the poor person would be only about one-third of what it is in figure 10.1. If the demand curves looked roughly like the ones I have drawn and the median voter was Mr 5, it is quite probable that the medical attention provided for the poor person would be approximately the same or better than the medical attention provided for the average-income person. Most assuredly it would be higher than that Mr 2 would provide for himself. Indeed, it would probably be higher than that available for Mr 3 and Mr 4.

Once again these assumptions are based on the view that in our society the demand curves have about the same shape as those shown for Mr 2 and Mr 3 in the diagram – that may not be true about the real world. It does seem to be true, however, that in those cases in which there is a sharp cutoff with free medical care being provided below a certain point and none above, there is always a group of voters whose incomes are just above the level at which they can get free medical attention and who will be irritated by the program. They will be paying for their own medicine and consuming less than the poor person, and at the same time paying through taxes for a sizable portion of his medical attention. The size of this group will depend on detailed assumptions, but it can very easily be quite large. Where we have graduated decline in the amount of medical service as incomes rise, much the same phenomenon occurs, but it is not quite as conspicuous. This point will be discussed at length below.

In reality in all societies, the providers of services have considerable influence on how much is provided, and the providers of the services in this case are the medical professions. They may be able to push the total provision high enough so that the indigents are receiving considerably more medical attention than is the average citizen. This is possible because the doctors, etc., are themselves likely to vote for increased provision to the poor not because they feel sympathetic towards the poor but because they want their own incomes raised. They will characteristically already have incomes well above average and the result may be that the poor, the doctors, and let us say the top 30 percent of the (nondoctor) population jointly make up the voting block which passes these high expenditures.

Note that in figure 10.1 the benefit to Mr 1 when we switch

from private provision to public provision is the trapezoidal area *abcd*. If he had simply been given $6 in cash it would have been the area *ae*03, and he would have been somewhat better off. Still, he receives an unambiguous gain in the shift from providing his own service to having the government provide it. In our next step, when we move to general medical care provided by the government, the poor will still be better off than they would be if they were providing it themselves, but they may well be worse off than under the situation of figure 10.1.

Universal Provision of Services

Consider figure 10.2, which shows the situation under universal provision of medical care. Once again the real cost is shown by a line marked "cost, real and to Mr 2," the cost to Mr 1 is shown by the "cost to Mr 1" line, and the cost to Mr 3 by the "cost to Mr 3" line. Note that in each of these cases the cost is three times as high as it was in figure 10.1 simply because the medical provision instead of being provided for one person is being provided for three persons.

The demand curve for Mr 1 is taken from figure 10.1. The demand curves for Mr 2 and Mr 3 now represent their demand for their own medical treatment plus whatever charitable desire they may have to provide medical treatment for Mr 1, since the only way they can do so under these circumstances is by increasing the total medical expenditure for everyone.

Let us begin our discussion by considering the effect on Mr 1 of this change. We pointed out that his welfare gain in moving from no government provision to government provision for the poor was only the area *abcd* on figure 10.1, which is represented on figure 10.2 by the area *abcd*. The median voter in this case is Mr 2 and the society will provide quantity *N* of medical attention. Mr 1 now gets more medical care than he got in figure 10.1 (although as mentioned earlier this is a mere artifact determined by the way the diagram has been drawn) but he has to pay more taxes. The amount in taxes he was paying on his previous medical attention is shown by the area under the dashed line near the bottom in the left-hand corner of figure 10.2. Since the total tax burden has gone up and since he is paying one-sixth of the amount, his total taxes

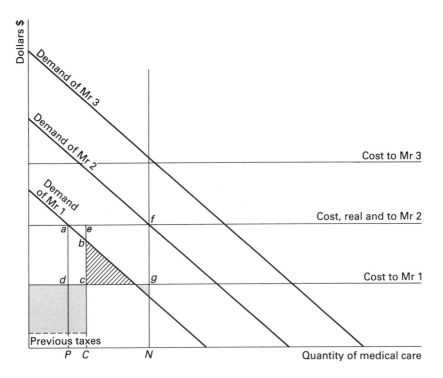

FIGURE 10.2 *Cost of medical care for three voters — rich (Mr 3), middle-class (Mr 2), and poor (Mr 1) — under universal provision of medical care. Dotted rectangle = additional taxes of Mr 1. Dotted triangle = loss from excessive medical care to Mr 1. Shaded triangle = gain from additional medical care for Mr 1.*
(Figure by University of Wisconsin Cartographic Laboratory.)

go up and he therefore suffers a loss through tax collection shown by the dotted rectangle. He has a further loss to the right near line N; the small dotted triangle is the additional medical attention which he receives which is not worth its tax cost to him. In the real world this little triangle might well not exist.

These losses, of course, are not the only effect. He also receives an unambiguous gain which is the shaded triangle. In the real world this triangle may not exist because he may already be receiving as much (or more) medical attention under the income-tested scheme as he will receive under the universal scheme. in figure 10.2, of course, his losses exceed his gains, but again, this may be attributed to the way the diagram was drawn.

The benefits which the poor receive depend on what we might call the degree of inadequacy of the medical attention that the poor receive. In this case "inadequacy" can't be defined technically because it depends on the total resources available at a given time. The real question is, Are the poor getting less than their per capita share of medical attention? Even that is not a fair question, because all of the empirical studies of national health services indicate that the poor, owing to their difficulty in filling out forms, poor motivation, and sometimes their difficulty in dealing with officials, get less than their share on a per capita basis of the medical resource of the society, even under theoretical "universalization." Let us say they get 90 percent of what a middle- or upper-class person would receive dealing with the same legal apparatus.

To clarify this issue, let us assume that some individual poor person has an income of $1,000 and was paying 1 percent of that or $10 as his share of the support of the income-tested health scheme. He received under this income-tested scheme $80 a year worth of medical attention. A government program is then adopted which provides $100 of medical attention for every citizen in the country. This means the total taxes used to pay for medicine will rise say five times, and because he is still paying his same allocated share of the cost,[5] he finds himself paying $50 in taxes. Even if he got the full $100 worth of treatment he would be worse off than he was before.[6] If we assume, realistically, that he actually gets only 90 percent of the national standard because of bureaucratic difficulties, he would be even worse off.

In this hypothetical case the individual would become better off only if the increase in medical attention he received nearly doubled the amount he had before (i.e. if the charitably provided medical care was only a little over one-half of the national standard). Further, even this would only be true if the marginal unit of medicine which he received was worth more to him than the taxes he paid on that marginal unit. Note that all of this depends on the exact numbers chosen. But I invite the reader to experiment with realistic numbers.

No one as far as I know has figured out how much the poor actually pay in taxes in the United States. Recent work has indicated that the tax incidence calculations that were used in the past are suspect. But let us stick to what we might call the Musgrave generalization, which holds that the actual taxes (not the taxes in my more expanded sense) that any person in our society below the highest income brackets pays are roughly proportional to his income. If this is so, the cost to the poor of going to universal programs is apt to be very considerable.

For the poor the increasing budget drain represented by universal medical care will not only raise the taxes they pay, it will also reduce the number of other income supplements which the state can give them. Thus, their taxes will go up and the other direct payments they recieve will go down. (Both of these items count as their increase in taxes.)

It is not generally realized that the expansion of one government program to aid the poor normally leads to the reduction of other such programs. There are two basic reasons. The first is simply that the government cannot spend an infinite amount of money, and thus an increase in budget on one item is likely to lead to at least some reduction in budgetary provision for other items. The second reason is that the reduction is particularly likely to occur in related items because members of Congress are likely to feel that if HHS receives generous funding for program A, it is only fair that part of the cost should come from HHS's program B.

Lindsay and Zycher's examination of distributional effects of the Canadian health plan find that "most of the cost of the Canadian National Health Insurance was borne by the economically disadvantaged."[7] There are a number of statistical problems with the Lindsay and Zycher work which, though a pioneering exploration of a completely new field, needs to be replicated in other areas. Nevertheless, it is the only empirical evidence on the point at this time.

Let us consider what happens in the real world. As I mentioned earlier, in the real world we have more people and a smaller part of the population is considered to be poor than the one-third in our three-citizen society. Thus, the level of provision under income-tested health provisions is apt to be farther to the right than we shown in figure 10.2. Indeed, it can be actually to the right of the level shown by line N. Under these extreme circumstances (which apparently existed in England when the National Health

Service was adopted) the poor receive a sizable welfare loss when we switch from income-tested to universal programs. Indeed, everyone except the poor and the wealthy gain from this shift and the poor are hurt. The people who gain most, however, are the near-poor (i.e, the people whose incomes are slighty above the income-test level); they now find that medicine is "free" and they can consume more of it.

Other aspects of the real world should also be mentioned here. One of them is that the transfer from an income-tested to a universal system does not increase the number of hospitals or doctors in society in the short run. Thus, at best it will lead to a rearrangement of the current medical resources with some people getting more and some people getting less. In the case of the British National Health Service for example, there was a very pronounced reduction in the resources available to the poor, with the result that during the period in which medicine was being revolutionized by introduction of antibiotics, the death rate of the poorest part of the English population actually rose.[8]

A Gradual Form of Income Testing

Let us now consider the situation where the income testing takes a gradual rather than abrupt form. In illustration let us assume that the state pays 100 percent of the medical care of people who are literally penniless and then reduces this percentage payment for medical care gradually until, let us say, the individuals had an income of $10,000, at which point the subsidy fell to 0. If this were converted to a universal program paid for by taxes, then the net effect would be to make the people at the bottom of the distribution worse off, because they now would pay at least some taxes that they didn't pay before and receive the same or fewer services.[9] It seems likely, as shown in figure 10.3 that the increase in medical services will begin to offset the rise in taxes at some fairly low income (I have arbitrarily chosen $2,500) and then remain above taxes to reach a maximum improvement at $5,000, with a gradual fall as the increase in the taxes comes closer to and eventually passes the benefits from free medical attention. The wealthy suffer most, and part of the group that we may arbitrarily

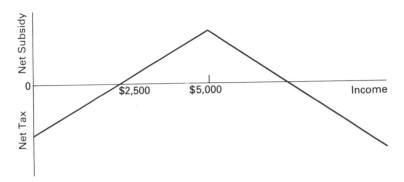

Figure 10.3 Costs of medical services as income increases in switch from a gradual income-tested program to a universal provision of medical care.

refer to as poor (but the upper end of the poor group), and part of the group that I call middle class gain.

Universalization of programs often is urged on the grounds that income-tested programs in fact do not reach all the poor. It is implied, although as far as I can see there is no evidence, that making the program available for the upper-income brackets will increase the number of poor people who avail themselves of it. Even if it were true, it would be an extraordinarily expensive way of increasing the number of poor people in the program. The poor people who do not participate in the program do not presumably because partly they really don't like the program, partly they have difficulty with the bureaucracy, and partly through mere ignorance. The first is not a problem since people who voluntarily and with full knowledge choose not to enter the program are presumably better off outside it. The second would not in any way be affected by universalizing the program since the red tape would probably be worse in a large program than a small program. The third calls for an advertising campaign and such a campaign would surely be immensely cheaper than extending the program to the whole population.

So far I have used an extremely restricted model. Not only does it have only three citizens, but I arranged the possible choice patterns so the system always has a simple straightforward equilibrium. In the real world we do observe that political activity tends to reach a stopping point and so there must be an equilibrium of some sort; however, there is not necessarily an equilibrium in the simple direct sense that we have discussed so far.

Empirical Evidence

Before turning to complicating our model by taking these matters into account, however, we briefly discuss some empirical evidence which indicates that the basic conclusions drawn so far are correct. This empirical evidence is unfortunately not very sophisticated, indeed it was drawn from ordinary observation and reading the newspapers, but I think the reader will be able to confirm it from his own experience.

The specific empirical evidence seems to show that the pressure for universalizing the medical program does not come from the poor but from the lower-middle class. Indeed, there is a very high correlation between pressure groups for universal medical care and pressure groups for raising the minimum wage. Since the minimum wage clearly hurts the poor, one has to deduce that these groups do not have the interest of the poor very strongly at heart. This does not mean, however, that no one else is in favor of a minimum wage. In the upper income groups, a number of people favor it partly through miscalculation of its effects on them and partly through genuinely charitable motives. There are also those among the poor who favor it. The real push, however, comes from organizations like the AFL/CIO, whose members might well benefit.

Better empirical evidence is needed, however, because all this empirical evidence indicates is that the principal beneficiaries of universalizing medical treatment will be the people who are just above the cutout line on income-tested medical provision for the poor. It does not prove that the poor do not in fact still gain.

Consumer Preference

So far we have simply calculated what the outcome would be under both an income-tested and a universal program. Let us now permit the three citizens to vote on the issue of which alternative they want, granting that they have already been told what these outcomes will be. Wealthy Mr 3 will clearly be in favor of the income-tested scheme. For the other two, Mr 1 and Mr 2, however, their choice depends on the exact details of the income-tested scheme. In the example from figure 10.2, Mr 2 would be in favor of the income-tested scheme but Mr 1 would not. The result, however, is heavily dependent on our specific assumptions.

From our current assumptions about taxes (i.e., that taxes are roughly proportional to income), it is clear that the exact location of the net payoff line in figure 10.3 depends, in part, on whether, in net, the program transfers funds from the poor. If it transfers funds from the poor, the payoff line will be higher than if the switch to universal medical attention leads to more resources being spent on the poor. When this line is shifted then, of course, the dividing line between the wealthy and the middle class also shifts. If we assume that the people vote in accordance with their interest, this shift changes the number of people voting for the universalization.

In general, if universalization actually transfers funds away from the poor, the category we have referred to as middle class will be larger and hence there will be more votes for the program, while if it transfers funds to the poor the category we call middle class will be smaller and the wealthy category will be larger and hence there will be fewer votes for the program. Of course, it is not only the middle class and wealthy who vote on the issue, the poor do also. If the poor favor universalization, then the loss of some of the voters from the middle class to the wealthy class by lowering the net payoff line would make little difference. The poor are about 10 percent of the population, they only need to have 41 percent of the remainder on their side to win.

The situation of the poor is ambiguous. First, we have pointed out that they gain considerably less from the universalization than the people in the lower end of the middle class. Second, it is quite possible they will lose, and third, it is extremely difficult to calculate exactly whether they will gain or lose.

The calculation problem is made even more difficult by the fact that almost all of the people who are experts in the field will be in favor of universalization because they will in one way or another gain if the service is universalized. The experts are apt to be either employees of the welfare service or potential employees or people who expect research grants from the welfare service, etc. There are occasional specialists in this field whose incomes do not either directly or indirectly originate in the welfare program itself, but their number is very small compared to the number of people who are specialists and whose incomes will actually increase whenever the welfare programs are expanded.

Thus, the possibility that the poor will lose out from the program is not likely to be emphasized very much, even if it is true. The poor are apt to be told they will gain whether they do or do not. They don't face an easy calculation problem like the lower-middle class and must depend on experts or learn to do rather complicated calculations themselves. Hence, they are liable to be deceived.

In this respect we have here only one example of a general problem of the poor in a democracy. People in general are poor because they are not too intelligent, lack motivation, etc. This not only makes them inept in a private marketplace, it also makes them inept in the political marketplace. Consequently, they tend to do poorly in the distribution of pork, which is such an important part of democratic politics. Perhaps as a result of their low general motivation or perhaps because they understand this situation, they tend to abstain from voting in any event. In general what they get out of democracy reflects not their real voting power, which tends to be wasted, but esentially charitable motives on the part of upper-income voters. These charitable motives, although real, do not seem to be very strong.

A Combined Package

But let me now complicate my model further. So far I have been assuming that the only points at issue are whether the health service shall be income tested or universal and the exact level at which the health service will be provided. Further, I have used a proportional tax system to finance the program. It is possible to combine either of these systems with different tax arrangements, with the result that the income shifts which I have been describing will not necessarily occur. For example, a switch from an income-tested to a universal program could be accompanied by an appropriate package of taxes so that even though it greatly increased the cost of the medical service, only the wealthy minority lost on the deal while everyone else gained.

It is fairly easy to demonstrate that such combined packages do not lead to any firm equilibrium. Suppose, for example, a bill were proposed that would provide the universal health care free and that a special tax to finance it was imposed, falling on only the top 49 percent of the population. We would have a 51 percent majority for the plan but the wealthy top 49 percent being clever people, could offer to some particular group of 2 percent of the population twice what they are getting under the universal health program with the result that they would favor this new proposal and the wealthy, of course, would favor it also because their taxes would fall. Their taxes would fall particularly sharply if they arranged that this new, and in total rather small, payment be financed only by the people in the bottom 51 percent who are not also in the 2 percent. We can go on with various combinations – each of which will beat the previous one. Any distribution of tax and benefit that you care to name can be reached by a properly planned set of proposals. When it comes to income distribution, there is in fact no equilibrium solution if all proposals are available.

In the real world things are fortunately a good deal more stable. In part this is unexplained, but there are a number of partial explanations for the observed reasonable stability of income redistribution measures.

Redistribution Effects

The first of these partial expalantions is the straightforward fact that income redistribution away from the wealthy pays more than income redistribution away from anyone else. There is simply more money there. The tax on the top 10 percent of the population has as its total possible yield more than a tax on any other 10 percent of the population. This being so, tax systems in a democracy have a strong tendency to fall particularly heavily on the wealthy. The proportional income tax which we have been using as our base and which except for the very top does not deviate too much from the reality in most democracies is, in fact, a tax which gets a good deal more money from the top 10 percent of the population than from any other bracket.

The transfer of funds from the wealthy, even though it is not a very large-scale phenomenon in absolute quantity, benefits mainly the middle class. When the poor are given special privileges, and they usually are in all societies, this reflects charity on the part of the middle class and wealthy rather than the political power of the poor. In any event, if we look at the actual history of the development of Social Security and other social welfare programs in the United States, it is fairly obvious that redistribution to the poor was not one of its major objectives.[10]

Medicare, a general program for all of the old, could be predicted to lead to a very sharp increase in the income of doctors and civil servants, not lower-income groups, and also a rearrangement of American medical resources in which the principal beneficiaries were older people who are not particularly poor. The older poor, were, of course, already receiving free medical attention. This increased demand for medical services combined with no increase in the number of doctors or hospitals in the short run surely meant that everyone else, including the poor, had a reduction in their medical care.

At the same time the Medicare was passed, Medicaid, an income-tested program which provided resources only for the poor, was also enacted. It seems likely for most of the poor that Medicaid counteracted the effect of Medicare. The net effect of the two programs was surely to benefit doctors and the older non poor. Whether the poor benefited or not is something which cannot be said for certain, but if they did benefit it was because of the existence of the income-tested program.

I would like to say that this phenomenon not only occurred in these two cases in the United States (and they are, of course, the two most significant examples of recent expansion in social welfare activity in the United States) but occurs always and everywhere. Unfortunately I cannot, because I simply don't know enough. Here again empirical research is called for and unfortunately it is an extremely difficult type of empirical research. Substantially each social welfare program in each country must be looked at in great detail with great care and with a good deal of skepticism for statements made by its apologists to see whether this is a general phenomenon or not. Once above I suggested a good project for a doctoral dissertation. Here we have a set of good projects for maybe 200 doctoral dissertations.

As a start on empirical research on this phenomenon, I should like to discuss three studies which I have succeeded in turning up. The first of these concerns Germany in the period 1969 through 1975, which was the initial period of the Social Democrat–Liberal coalition government. This government passed a considerable number of redistributional laws and increased the size of the transfer sector quite considerably. Martin Pfaff's study of this period shows a net increase in inequality.[11] The increased transfers, even though enacted by a basically left-wing government, benefited the middle and upper classes rather than the poor. This study is particularly notable because Pfaff's predilections are quite in the other direction.

That the same phenomenon has occurred in Britain under its current (1978) Labour government is indicated by an article in the London *Economist*. Between 1974 and 1976, a period in which once again a new left-wing (Labour) government was enacting very large increases and rearrangements in the social welfare program in England, the number of poor in England almost doubled.

My third bit of evidence comes from Switzerland, where there are direct public votes on many issues. Werner Pommerehne has chosen a number of communes in Basel and examined the redistributional effect of direct popular voting on budgets.[12] These votes were not all specifically on social welfare programs but they did have considerable distributional impact. Pommerehne's study raises a certain number of difficulties with respect to the definition of transfer or nontransfer patterns of taxation and expenditure. It is, however, clear from the results of his study that there is, at the very least, no strong tendency to transfer funds to the poor when the populace is permitted to vote directly on such issues.

As a last item, and here we go to the underdeveloped world, two Indian scholars, Jagannadahm and Palvia, calculated the Gini coefficient for government employees and then for the pensioners (i.e., retired government employees).[13] They found that the Gini coefficient for the actual employees was much lower than for the pensioners. The apparent explanation is that inflation has tended to lower pensions and the existing power holders in India, whether they are the civil servants, or legislatures, have raised the wages and improved the pension prospects of active civil servants while letting the pensions of the already retired personnel deteriorate. This is not directly relevant to the income-testing hypothesis, but it is in general accord with Pommerehne's results. The legislature and civil service of India are much more concerned with their own well being and with middle-income groups than with the poor and elderly pensioners.

Of course these are merely a set of samples. They are, however, the only ones I could find in which the subject had been discussed at all. I cannot say on the basis of this evidence that the phenomenon is general but I suspect it is.

The Politics of Income Testing

In any event, if it is very general that universal programs benefit the middle class and not the poor, it is not difficult to explain, and certainly it is not difficult to explain the case of the United States. People who are interested in expanding social welfare systems from income-tested to universal programs are characteristically interested in just that and not particularly in helping the poor. Establishing the program requires political support which almost of necessity has to come from the group that we have referred to as the middle class because that is the only group which makes an unambiguous gain. This group will be smaller and less enthusiastic about a program designed to increase the benefits of the poor considerably, because there is simply that much less left for them.

Hence, people trying to introduce some kind of general health insurance are not likely to propose a program which will transfer funds from the middle class to the poor. There is another alternative, however, which is to finance it in such a way as to transfer funds from the wealthy, preferably the truly wealthy not just the people whom I have denominated wealthy in my somewhat arbitrary category. The trouble with this plan is that the richest group is probably the best informed, most politically influential group in the electorate. Futher, it is fairly small group and hence able to organize much more efficiently than larger groups.

In general to try to get anything through Congress you should try to avoid antagonizing any sector of the population. Now, of course, there are things put through Congress despite disadvantaging specific groups; our whole energy program for example. But on the whole, this is something you would want to avoid. The national health program will be easier to put through Congress if the cost doesn't fall too conspicuously on the wealthy. On the other hand, if the cost doesn't fall too conspicuously on the wealthy, then it must fall on the middle class or on the poor. The proponents of the program then are likely to set up financing methods which lead to the whole program being mildly regressive.

It should be noted that insofar as the middle-class voters can succeed in getting funds from the wealthy, there is no obvious reason why they should pass them on to the poor. Thus, even if we do have a scheme which raises the cost to the upper-income groups, like the recent extension of the social security tax to all wages, there is no reason to believe that the poor rather than the middle class will benefit.

This last line of reasoning, while I find it persuasive, is clearly much less rigorous than the models I have used before. I have difficulty imagining how it could be tested. Detailed historical research of the sort that Carolyn Weaver did on the origins of the Social Security Act would be called for and unfortunately this type of historical investigation has the characteristic that it is always possible for different historians to disagree.[14]

Conclusion

Any extension of social welfare activity provides a direct benefit to those who receive it and a direct cost on those who are paying for it. Those who are paying for it may well be the recipients, but in any event we have to net out the two sides of the budget. This is, of course, particularly important when we are contrasting an income-tested with a non-income-tested program, because the improvement in quality (if there is an improvement at all) for the people who have previously been receiving the income-tested service is apt to be much less than the gain obtained by people who were previously not receiving it because the income test barred them.

The third item that has to be netted out, of course, is the cost to the former recipients of the income-tested service, in that the additional budgetary cost of spreading the service over the population as a whole probably will mean that various other services which they would be entitled to either are contracted or at at least not expanded as rapidly as they otherwise would be. Only when we have completed this rather difficult computation can we tell whether the people who previously received the income-tested service benefit or are injured by the expansion to the society as a whole.

Fortunately, the calculations for the rest of the society are a good deal easier, although here again all three of these items are present. They will receive a benefit, they will pay taxes, and presumably the existence of this program will have effects elsewhere in the government budget that will benefit or injure them. In either case, however, it is usually fairly easy to at least work out the direction of the effects. With the poor the problem is much more difficult.

The calculation above, of course, involves simply the measurement of effects. When we consider the political forces which may lead to the expansion of a program it is, in general, clear that if people who are interestd in expanding the program are trying merely to help the poor, they have chosen an inept way of doing it. Only if they feel that they can trick members of the middle and upper class into voting for a program to help the poor by that indirect method which is more generous than they are willing to give in a direct and open way, is it sensible. Politics, of course, involves a great deal of misinformation and a great deal of trickery and so the possibility that this is true cannot be totally ruled out, but it seems to me unlikely. It will not escape the reader that I personally think that in most of the cases in which income-tested programs have been converted into universal programs, the poor have been injured, and indeed that this is what was intended. I tend to think of them as programs which are aimed at benefiting the group which I have referred to as the middle class and in addition benefiting the factor suppliers – the doctors, welfare workers, professors of social work, etc. who will gain when such programs are extended.

I suspect that the other authors in this book feel quite differently on the subject. Indeed, I must compliment Professor Garfinkel on his willingness to bring in what he must think of as a particularly perverse reactionary in order to present the other side.[15] I trust, however, that the reader, having read my paper, will agree that even if my personal opinion on the matter is wrong, at any event the problem is in fact a difficult one and the matter would deserve a great deal of careful empirical study.

11

A (Partial) Rehabilitation of the Public Interest Theory

From the earliest work in Public Choice, scholars have tended to assume that the public interest is not a major theme in the operation of government, certainly in democratic government. In a way, this was a sensible and desirable reaction to the dominance of public interest type thinking in traditional political science. Further, public interest defined as abstract devotion to the public good is probably of little importance in politics. There is, however, another more restricted meaning of public interest in which it is of considerable importance and it is this restricted meaning that I intend to discuss.

If we look at active governments, we see that they engage in a large number of activities whose benefit is not narrowly focused on certain small groups or individuals. Military establishments are an obvious example. There are no doubt manufacturers of military equipment who gain from increased military appropriations and the soldiers themselves, of course, gain from raising of wages, but the bulk of the population vote for or against such military machines, without any direct special interest in them. There are then, at least some cases of public interest voting. Further, if we consider even the special interest groups, let us say farmers who want higher prices for wheat, we can easily demonstrate that any individual farmer would be better off if he did nothing and let his fellow farmers take on the expense of influencing the government. We do observe individual farmers doing just that, but we also observe a fair amount of pressure being brought to bear on congressmen in such areas. This, from most of our standpoints is regarded as a public bad, but from the standpoint of the small group that will benefit, it is a public good. Here again, I think that we must include some explanation of this kind of public interest activity in a complete theory of politics.

I do not want, of course, to quarrel with the existing literature here. In deed, the problems involved in generating public goods, which were so powerfully outlined in Olson's pioneering book, are fully accepted. I do want to explain, however, why the voters we describe in Public Choice theory will vote for such public interest matters as national defense, government farm programs, and a police force.

A very clear-cut (and traditional) reason why voters might be motivated to put the public interest into their decision process is simply that most people are, to some extent, charitable and interested in helping others. This affects their voting behavior as well as their private behavior. An individual who is trying to help others may do so, in part, by voting for some public good, even though he doesn't expect to benefit from it himself. He may also choose to make charitable gifts through the government.

It should not be necessary to point out that although this is a genuine motive it is not a very strong one. In private life people are willing to give away perhaps, 5 per cent of their incomes to help the poor or other worthy causes. There is no reason to believe that in politics they are any more charitable. In fact, if we look at the modern welfare state and observe how much of the national income is, in fact, given to the poor, it normally turns out to be markedly less than five per cent.

But here two problems, the tendency of the particular expenditure to be diverted by selfish interest and poor information, are important. The special self-interest of particular groups of people who would like to be subjects of charity, and more importantly of those civil servants and others who are engaged in the process of distributing the charity or producing the public interest activities are always important here. I suspect that for a great many people the Kennedy Center, in Washington, is thought of as a sacrifice which we are willing to make for the public good. There is no doubt, however, that for the people directly involved in it, it is a selfish interest and that they devoted a good deal of time and energy to making certain that it was bent in their direction.

As a more topical example, the National Fund for the Humanities is intended to generate higher culture for the United States, an objective which we know from history of such things as symphony orchestras, opera companies and museums, that individuals are willing to endow out of essentially charitable motives. It has, however, developed a group of people who are dependent on it and recent proposals to cut it have been opposed by fairly straightforward client groups. In this case, it should be said that bad information is very important in continuing the support of the Fund. If the average voter knew the kind of "art" that is in fact supported, he would most assuredly vote against it. This may, of course, indicate that the average voter is not as artistic as the civil servants who run the program, but in any event that is his attitude. So much for what you might call pure public good reasoning. There is another, and I think very large area where the voter may vote in terms of the "public interest" because, in essence, that is the only thing he can do. He has no selfish interest in the matter. In order to discuss it, let me take a brief digression away from preference aggregation to an area where we are attempting to determine what is, rather than what people like. Specifically, let us consider judicial administration.

We make every effort to see to it that judges and juries have no material interest in the matters they try. The idea is that they should be completely unbiased. Granted that they have no interest, one might inquire how they make up their mind. The answer must, of necessity, be that they do what they think is right because they have no countervailing motive. This system can be criticized. Surely if they had a motive to reach the right decision, they would put more energy and thought into their decisions than if we simply deprive them of all motive to go wrong. But to say that this can be criticized is not to offer any constructive suggestions for improvements. We do use this technique.

The point of this digression has been that this same technique is through accident, not through planning, an important aspect of democratic politics. The average voter making up his mind as to how he shall vote in any given election has absorbed, by way of TV and the newspapers, some information. The knowledge that he has about the current issues in the campaign is apt to be rather sporadic and inaccurate, but one characteristic that is fairly certain to be true most of the time is that most of the issues that seem to divide the candidates will be issues in which he either has no selfish motive himself or, alternatively, ones in which although he might have a selfish motive if he thought about the matter carefully, he has not thought about the matter carefully and doesn't intend to. At the conscious level he has no selfish motive.

To take a particularly clear-cut example,[1] one of the Western states recently had a referendum on a bill which would permit individuals selling their houses to, if they wished, refuse to sell the house to practicing homosexuals. It seems to have gotten a good deal of newspaper publicity and was, in fact, voted down in the referendum. Surely there were very few people in the district who voted on this particular issue because they had any selfish motives. Presumably, some homosexuals want to make it easier to purchase homes, but this must have been a very, very small minority of those who voted on the bill. The bulk of the people voting on this particular issue must have been primarily concerned with what they vaguely thought was the public interest.

This is, of course, an extreme example. But anyone reading the newspapers about any election, or for that matter almost any referendum, must quickly realize that the bulk of the people voting on any given issue have no particular selfish motive to be concerned with many issues. They will vote in terms of the public interest.

We do not here, however, want to be naive. In the average election, although most of the issues which are given great emphasis in the press and hence come to the attention of the average voter, are issues that do not affect him particularly in any direct selfish way, i.e., not measures in which he can be regarded as himself a member of a special interest bloc, there are some such cases in almost every election. Further, it seems likely that most voters are apt to pay more attention to these special issues than to the more general issues in which they have no direct interest. Thus the concentration of interest on special interest legislation is, I think, perfectly sensible. But we should not deduce from it that general interest or public interest considerations are totally without weight in politics.

The individual who simply absorbs information through the newspapers and then makes his decision on voting is not likely to be very well informed about any aspect of politics, but is apt to have heard more about those issues which don't affect him particularly than the issues which specially affect him. Thus he may end up voting, to some extent, on what he thinks is public interest rather than his own selfish interests.

This factor is to a considerable extent counterbalanced if we consider the situation of a congressman who is considering how to vote, with careful attention as to how that will affect the next election by the fact that there are specialized channels of information for those people who are members of interested minorities, and these specialized channels of information are likely to produce information to the small group of voters who are particularly interested in it. Nevertheless, the congressman must, of necessity, look at both sides of the ledger. We observe this fairly directly from the fact that there are no straightforward open transfers of funds to special interest minorities. We do not see a general and small tax used to pay cash sums to small minorities. This would be too blatant. We do see governments engaging in activities which are intended to generate public goods but which, in fact, do not. It is highly probable than the average citizen of almost any democracy thinks that a firm price control would be a good idea in order to end inflation. We periodically observe governments responding to this kind of pressure by enacting such price controls. Why they do so is not hard to understand. Indeed, granted the motives of a politician, the difficult question is why they ever repeal price controls. This is a case in which individuals badly informed are under the mistaken impression that a particular type of government policy is in the public interest when, as a matter of fact, it is not.[2]

Before leaving these cases in which the voter votes pretty consciously in the public interest, I perhaps should say a little about the information conditions. When he is deliberately acting charitably in his vote, he probably has at least some motive to become well informed about the specific charitable act. This does not mean he will be well informed but he won't be hopelessly badly informed. In those cases in which he is driven to vote in the public interest simply because he has no selfish interest, he has even weaker motives to become well informed. This is the area where casual fads, fancies, and fashions are particularly important in democratic politics. Thus, the "public interest" vote is very apt to be very badly informed.

So much for genuine public interest. We now turn to two areas where individuals vote in a way which to the outside observer might appear to represent the public interest, but where their actual motives are selfish. We should, of course, not oversimplify. The person who is genuinely interested in doing good may also vote in the same way that the selfish person in these areas does, and it is likely that for most people the two motives are, at least to some extent, intermingled.

We shall begin with technological public goods. Consider the army, for example. It is, on the whole, impossible for an individual to vote for his own interest without voting for that of others at the same time. Thus, if I thought that the Vietnamese war was important to defend me,[3] the only way I could vote for it would tend to produce the same "good" for all other people too.

This is, in general, true with respect to military activities. The economies of scale are so immense that individuals are unable to do much on their own and, hence, any decision that they make has to be collective. Under the circumstances, my completely selfish desire to have strong military protection has the by-product that I will protect other people. In other words, I will vote in such a way as to generate a public good. There are a number of activities of this sort – the police, the highway net, the weather bureau, or a patent system, are all examples.

We immediately note that in all of these cases, in addition to these very general drives for the "public interest," there are narrow interests also involved. I do not believe, however, that these narrow interests can be regarded as dominating the political process here. They bend the political process in various ways, but without the overwhelming "public interest" vote, these various goods would not be provided.

There is another collection of government services which are not technologically public, but where from the voter's standpoint it is much like the army, etc. They are goods or services that are technologically private but where the government can be used to provide them if large numbers of voters vote for them. Suppose, for an example, a special tax on a group of people used to pay pensions to another group of people. From all of these people's standpoint these are private goods or bads. Nevertheless, no individual could anticipate that he would receive his pension unless other people voted for it, too, and hence there would be no point in his voting for a pension for himself alone. He is apt to treat this large collection of private goods as if they were a public good. In practice, I suspect that this kind of thing is much commoner in modern political structure than true technological public goods. Of course, many, many cases are intermediate between the two.

Here again, one must expect that individuals, although basically voting for or against such programs with full awareness of the fact that it affects many other people, would do their best to bend it in their own direction. In this respect it is like the public goods. Just as the arms manufacturer hopes that the defense appropriation will largely be spent on buying his particular product, so the old age pensioner feels that, let us say, a special adjustment in the old age pension for the exceptionally high cost of living in his section of the country would be desirable.

To anticipate later discussion, the individual who votes in the way we are describing here has little motive to become well informed. He may cast a vote intending to increase his pension which will actually reduce it because he doesn't understand the complex actuarial calculations necessary to fully predict the outcome of his vote. Further, in general, it will not be worth his time to learn to understand such calculations, with the result that such ignorance is apt to be permanent. This again, will be discussed further after we have dealt with some other reasons why people might vote in the public interest.

Nevertheless, such programs as social security politically have all of the standard characteristics of a public good. Of course, we can readily find cases in which a public good is considered good or bad by large numbers of people, for example, the defense appropriation. We can also find cases where a private good is primarily pushed by a small group of people. The standard pork barrel project is obviously such a case.

There is, of course, an intermediate situation in which individuals face a public good for a small group. Suppose, for example, the farmers, as they have in the United States, approach the government and suggest the government raise the price of their products. This is, for the individual farmers, a public good although a public good that surely does not extend to the entire population. Its cost, on the other hand, does extend to practically the entire population and so is a public bad, although apparently most of the population doesn't know that it exists.

Looking at the matter entirely from the standpoint of the voter, the special interest is really no different from general interest. Mr Smith has preferences A through M for various subjects. Two of them are matters of very special interest to him and the others are of things which are, or at least he thinks are, matters of public interest. From Smith's standpoint his vote for a candidate will have as much effect on any one of these subjects as on any other. It is only if he personally evaluates one more strongly than others that he will give it additional weight.

It is often thought that the individuals in a pressure group can, somehow or other, get more out of their vote by voting for the special interest than for the public interest. This is not true. A vote is a vote is a vote. There is something to be gained for members of a pressure group by developing a reputation of being highly reliable and always selling their vote to the highest bidder on one particular subject and ignoring all others. An individual who chooses not to do so, however, will normally not have any significant effect on the prospect of this group's promise being believed next time. Our data on elections are far too imprecise to be able to detect an individual switch and, in any event, the individual would be of little interest to the congressmen.

It should be said here that from the congressmen's standpoint a special interest would be simply something that interests a concentrated group of voters rather than substantially everybody. It would not necessarily conform to the view of public goods held by economists. Let us return to the legislation permitting individual discrimination against homosexuals in selling houses. Presumably, this was pushed by a small intense group. From the politician's standpoint they are just as much a special interest group as people who want the harbor of their city dredged.

It is likely that, on the whole, if we look at those public goods that the government does generate, a great many of them are thought of by the politicians as concessions to various special groups. For a very long period of time the veterans' organizations in the United States pushed hard for increased military appropriations.[4] They were, I am sure, thought of by politicians as a special interest that had to be conciliated by large appropriations. In this case, of course, they were pushing for something which had much wider public support than would, for example, making Tulsa a deep water port, but the fact remains that from the politicians' standpoint they were a special interest.

Looking at the voters from the standpoint of the politician, there are a large number of people who have interests in various issues and these interests are of varying degrees of intensity. He attempts to choose a location in the multi-dimensional issue continuum which maximizes the probability of his being elected, granted that he has an opponent who will be trying to do the same thing. This means he must take into account the intensity of preference as well as the actual direction of preference on all issues.

It also means he must take into account the information conditions facing the voters. This leads to various tradeoffs in which he may take a position which is generally but not very strongly opposed and strongly favored by a special group, more often than not, small.

It is not by any means obvious, however, that only small groups have strong preferences. The Swiss government, for example, has never proposed simply abolishing its military machine which, on a per capita basis, is probably the most powerful in the world. If it did, I suspect they would find that substantially the entire population of Switzerland was intensely and vigorously opposed. Because of the widespread use of the referendum technique in Switzerland, intense minorities have less power and importance than they do in purely representative democracies. Still, intense minorities which are small enough so as not to attract the attention of the country as a whole regularly get all sorts of special privileges out of the Swiss government by a virtue of, in essence, threatening contrary votes at the next election.[5]

In the more normal type of democracy in which referendum is not as important as in Switzerland, it is likely that intense minorities do much better, simply because they are more likely to affect an elected politician thinking about the next election two years from now than they are to affect public opinion in general.

Looking at the matter in general terms, it is clear that from the voter's standpoint the distinction between public goods and private goods is not particularly relevant. Consider the social security administration. This is simply a very large collection of private goods and bads with individuals who anticipate their taxes to be greater than their receipts getting a private bad and individuals who have the opposite expectation getting a private good. In this respect it is like most transfers.[6] This is, however, a case in which we would anticipate very large numbers of people holding preferences of varying degrees of intensity one way or the other. For an alternative which is on quite the other extreme, suppose a proposal to censor some local pornography source. The groups favoring and opposing this would probably be rather small in spite of its "publicness."

These subtle distinctions are of little or no interest to the voter who simply makes up a list of thing he favors and opposes, determines which candidate favors each one, and then weighs them according to his intensity. They are also of no great importance to the politician who is simply interested in the effect of his decision on any given issue on the vote he will receive in the next election. He doesn't care whether the reason people favor or oppose a particular vote is the existence of public good or private good. He is, of course, interested in the number of people who are on each side of any issue and how strongly they feel. In particular, how likely they are to remember the whole thing at the next election and either reward or penalize him.

The way this works in politics is that the political entrepreneur who, let us assume, is somebody running for congress who makes up a platform of various proposals which he will push and, of course, emphasizes his previous record if he has one, as evidence of what he is likely to do. He attempts to design this in such a way that it will get him at least a majority of votes against his opponent. This means that he engages in what we called implicit logrolling, i.e., he balances a special provision for voter A which he knows voter A wants a great deal against two or three things which he knows voter A opposes, but which voter A doesn't feel very strongly about. The result of this mechanism is that is apt to make up a platform which consists of certain issues which he believes are widely supported, together with a large collection of other issues each of which is distinguished by an intense minority on the side which he favors and a relatively moderate majority on the other side. If he has done his job well, he will be elected.

Once the congressman gets into congress he is in a position where he should attempt more or less the same pattern, but in this case he is trying to create not a set of promises for the future but a pattern of behavior which will lead people to reelect him. For this purpose it is important for him to be able to say that he has gained things for his constituency. It is also important for him to be able to say that he has voted with the majority of his constituents on these issues where the majority is likely to know what has happened, and to be interested in the matter. Thus his pattern of behavior will, in this case, tend to follow not the implicit logrolling pattern described above but an explicit logrolling pattern in which he actually makes trades with other congressmen on various issues.

The result of this pattern is likely to be something like the American defense appropriation process. Most congressmen will be in favor of that amount of defense which is favored by the majority of their constituents. There is also a very strong desire on their part to see to it that defense expenditures are made in such a way as to benefit each individual constituency. For the first, it is not terribly difficult to get a general majority position in congress. For the second, an elaborate procedure of logrolling is put in train with the result that we have the pattern of military bases that we now observe.[7]

Let us consider the information conditions confronting the average voter. First, he has very little motive to become informed unless, for one of a variety of reasons, he actually likes to know something about politics. Information that he picks up casually from the press and the TV is not likely to be very profound and will, to a large extent, depend on current fashions and fads. If he does have some specific subject in which he is interested as a sort of a hobby, he may be very well informed on this but the number of such voters is small enough so that they probably have no effect on politics.

The very well worked out proofs that the average voter has no instrumental motive to become informed about things of public interest will not in any way be denied here. He may have the motive to become, at least to some extent, well informed on matters which will affect some small group of which he is a member. There his vote has a greater impact. Still, the motive is not likely to be high.

Thus, his information situation tends to exaggerate the effects we have discussed above. There is one particular area, the special interest legislation area, where his information lack is apt to be particularly appalling. Those special interest acts now being pushed politically, which inflict a very small cost on him in order to provide a large benefit to some concentrated minority, are probably totally unknown to him. If he does learn about them, he is apt to pick up some deceptive cover story circulated by the special interest group. Here we intellectuals could make a real contribution. If we simply educate the populace on the actual costs of these things, we would find that the bulk of them would not go through. Unfortunately, historically intellectuals have tended to favor large collections of special interest legislation, with the result that, if anything, they have contributed to the deception.

It should, of course, be pointed out when talking about special interest legislation that the individual is probably totally uninformed about the very large number of opportunities for special benefit to himself. The number of special interest groups that actually exist is probably but a tiny fraction of the potential total for such groups. The problems so well outlined by Mancur Olson meant that in most cases a special interest group is never organized. The initial investment of capital in informing the members of the group that they have common interests, inventing a cover story which will permit it to be passed through congress, and then getting the bill passed depend on individuals within the pressure group behaving in a way which is, from the standpoint of that pressure group, publicly interested. We do not expect that they will and, hence, only a very small portion of potential public interests in fact become politically viable. This is a very fortunate fact.

To sum up, the purpose of this paper has been to argue that Public Choice should not totally ignore public interest or public interest voting. It should certainly not ignore issues where there are very large numbers of people, all of whom have a private interest that points in the same direction. It is likely that the extremely forceful article by Samuelson, in which he presented the argument for public provision of public goods, has misled the students in this field.[8] The government does provide public goods but it also provides many other things. Basically, it provides things in a democracy for which a majority of the people will vote. This does not mean they will vote for each individual item but that the whole package is attractive to them.

This package includes a certain number of things that we readily recognize as public good. It also includes a large number of matters in which a small minority is interested, but interested very intensely, such as the standard logrolling issues. Last but by no means least, it includes private goods which are provided for by the government because their provision requires the use of coercion. Transfers are the most obvious example. This last category of private goods can be those that benefit fairly small but intense minorities or programs that benefit very large groups of people, like the various "welfare" programs first introduced by Bismarck in Imperial Germany. The tendency to completely overlook the public interest legislation and public interest motive, and even more completely to overlook large scale transfers as a motive for government activity should, I think, be changed. I do not, of course, want to argue that public interest is the dominant motive in politics but it is a motive.

12

How to Do Well While Doing Good!

Economic research always has the potential of contributing to public welfare since improved knowledge can have an effect on the world that is desirable and is unlikely to have an effect that is undesirable. Nevertheless, I would estimate that the average article in economic journals these days has very little prospect of contributing to the well-being of the world. Most economists know this and worry more about publication and tenure than about the contribution their research will make to public welfare. The argument of this chapter is that virtue does not have to be its own reward. The average economist can benefit his career while simultaneously making a contribution to the public welfare.

Consider, for example, the case of the dissolution of the Civil Aeronautics Board (CAB) in 1937, Congress cartelized the US air transport industry, establishing a government agency, the CAB, to supervise and control the cartel. As a result, in the United States air transportation prices were held well above their equilibrium, even though they were lower than the prices charged internationally and in Europe.[1]

In 1984, the CAB was abolished, and it is clear that economists played a major part in its destruction. A group of economists (Jim Miller is the one that I know best) devoted a great deal of time and effort to economic research in connection with the airline industry and to what we may call public relations activities in connection with it. They formed an improbable political alliance between the American Enterprise Institute and Senator Kennedy for the purpose of bringing the control device to an early grave. Further, they were able to convince some of the airlines that they would gain from the elimination of the CAB.

As far as I can see, when the economists began their campaign there was substantially no public interest in the matter at all; most people and politicians would have argued that the CAB was necessary in order to prevent the airlines from exploiting the passengers. It is also true that most of the economists who looked at the problem had approved the regulation. It should be said that a good many of the economists that looked at it were members of that small subset of the profession who were professional public utility economists and whose own personal income depends very heavily on the continued existence of these boards for which they can give expert testimony. Miller could have joined this small group but chose the other side, and in view of his subsequent career, it is hard to argue that he was not right, both from the standpoint of the public interest and his own career.

I do not want to, indeed am not competent to, go into the detailed history of this successful campaign, but I should like to point out two important factors: the first is that the average citizen, if he or she had known the truth about the CAB, would always have been opposed to it. This is one of the reasons why you can argue that it was in the public interest. The second is that it was not too hard to get the actual story out. The problem was mainly that of explaining the matter to the politician and the media. This is not necessarily easy since neither of these groups have any particular motive to think hard about the true public interest. They are both much more interested in the image of public interest currently in the minds of the citizenry. But to say that it is not easy, is not to say that it is impossible, and here we have a clear-cut case where it was accomplished. The theme of this sermon is "Go Thou and Do Likewise."

The CAB is not by any means the only example. Banking regulation has to a large extent collapsed in recent years. This was to a considerable extent the result of technological developments, but the existence of a vigorous group of economic critics of the regulations was no doubt important. After all, the regulators could have just changed their regulations to take in the new technology. The fact that they did not was certainly, to some extent, the result of the work of the antiregulation economists in this area. The partial deregulation of the tracking industry is almost entirely the result of economic activity and, indeed, during the latter part of the Carter administration an economist was acting chairman of the ICC.[2]

In all of the cases originally the majority of the economic profession was on the wrong side, *favoring* regulation. This is one of the problems we face when we talk about economists having a good effect on policy. We must admit that in the past economists have frequently had a bad effect. Good economists have always had a good effect, however, and those who had a bad effect were bad economists. This is not just an ad hoc argument; I believe that one can look into the matter and discover that the people who favored such agencies as the ICC at the time they were set up were markedly poorer economists than the ones who objected to it.

There are other striking examples. In 1929 the United States was probably the world's highest tariff nation. It is true that during the intervening years we have developed a habit of setting up quotas and voluntary agreements, but even if you add those on, we still are a very low trade barrier nation. This change seems to be almost entirely an outcome of steady economic criticism. Certainly, it is very hard to put your finger on any other reason for the change.

Once again however, the history is not clear. The protective tariff, of course, has long been a bête noire of the economists, but a review of the advanced theoretical literature over the last years shows far more discussion of optimal tariffs than of the desirability of getting rid of tariffs. This is particularly surprising because the articles dealing with optimal tariffs rarely, if ever, point out that their optimality is a rather special one and that, in any event, it would be impossible to calculate an optimal tariff in the real world.[3] Still, the majority of economic opinion was always against protective tariffs even if this point of view did not get much attention in the technical journals. In a way the success of the tariff-lowering movement depended a great deal on the fact that the secretary of state for some 12 years was a former Southern congressman who had learned free trade in his youth and stuck with it. Cordell Hull, of course, has been dead for many years, but the trend that he started continued. Certainly, the general favorable economic climate for such cuts was important there.

What can we do now and, more specifically, what can readers do that is good but will also help them in their careers? My argument is that there are numerous instances that almost all economists can agree are rent-seeking and detract from general welfare. In such cases virtue need not be its own reward.

An Example of an Anti-rent-seeking Argument

Let me begin with an example on which almost all economists would agree. There are about 300 British Columbian egg producers, and some time ago it occurred to them that they were not as wealthy as they would like to be. They pressed the British Columbia government into setting up the British Columbia Egg Control Board, a cartel in which the government not only fixed prices but actually engaged in civil service employing operations. Specifically, the Egg Control Board purchased the eggs from the owners of egg factories and then sold them to the public.

The original arguments for this program (other than that it would make the egg producers wealthy), were that they would stabilize prices and protect the "family farm." They have stabilized prices. If you compare prices in British Columbia to those in Washington State, which has roughly the same conditions, it is clear they fluctuate more in Washington State. However, they have stabilized prices primarily by preventing the falls in price that periodically cause so much distress for producers of eggs in Washington. Whether this particular kind of stability is admired by the housewife, as opposed to the egg producer, is not perfectly clear. As for protecting the "family farmer," I doubt that these enterprises really should be referred to as family farms, but it is true that there is some evidence that the average size is possibly slighty suboptimal in British Columbia.

In order to charge a monopoly price it is, of course, necessary to prevent entry into the business. This is done by the traditional grandfather clause, so that those who were producing eggs in British Columbia when the scheme started are the only ones who are permitted to do so. As a result, the wealth of the farmers has increased very greatly because the permits to produce eggs are now valuable. Indeed, for the average egg producer, the permit is more than half his total capitalization.

It should be pointed out, however, that in addition to the egg producers there is one other beneficiary of this scheme. The egg producers produce more eggs than can be sold in British Columbia at what the British Columbia Egg Marketing Board thinks is a stable price. The additional eggs are sold on the international market for conversion to things like dried eggs at whatever the market will bring.

How do I know all of this about the British Columbia Egg Marketing Board? The answer is simple. Two economists decided that it would be a worthwhile study and the Fraser Institute published it in the form of a small booklet.[4] Borcherding and Dorosh thus acquired a reasonably good publication, probably quite easily. It is no criticism of the pamphlet to say that it involves no particular economic sophistication or advanced techniques. It may have been a little difficult, because I presume the Egg Board was not exactly enthusiastic about cooperating with them. Nevertheless, I would imagine that the cost–benefit analysis of this pamphlet, in terms of getting a publication and the effort put into it, was very exceptionally favorable. Further, the pamphlet itself certainly will make the survival of the Egg Board, at least, a little less certain, a result most economists believe would be beneficial.

Of course I hope that more is done here. The pamphlet was published by the Fraser Institute, which exists essentially for the purpose of doing this kind of thing and attempting to influence public policy by its research. The head of the Fraser Institute frequently appears on television. I would think that the prospects for the Egg Board are clearly worse than they were before all of this started. I hope that Borcherding and Dorosh follow up on this, not so much by further research, although that of course probably can be done, as by trying to get other publications in the local media.

Here, I am going to suggest that they do something unprofessional; I believe economists should make an active effort to interest the local newspaper and other media in such issues. Stories of a small entrenched interest robbing the general public are the kinds of stories that do go well once you convince a reporter. Further, they are not particularly complicated.

Such activities are not the ones economists normally engage in; moreover, it will be a little difficult to interest newspaper reporters. Newspaper reports tend simply to say what other newspaper reports have said.[5] Granted that reporters behave this way, they are nonetheless normally looking for a scandal which they can make headlines about, and there are innumerable examples. The licensing of private yacht salesmen in California is my favorite case of the public being protected against low commission rates, but I am sure most economists can think of a half dozen more. But let us defer further discussion of general publicity for now.

We can roughly divide various rent-seeking activities for which there is likely to be a consensus among economists that they are indeed rent-seeking into three categories: those that involve spending money in a way that in the standpoint of the average taxpayer is foolish but that benefits a particular group, those that involve fixing prices above equilibrium, and those that involve obtaining cartel profits by restricting entry into a business.[6]

Economists have not been very successful in their efforts to stop federal government expenditures resulting from rent-seeking. Jack Hirshleifer, for example, devoted a good deal of time and energy, together with a number of experts in the field, in attempting to prevent the Feather River Project from being built in California. It has not been completed yet, but, on the whole, their efforts cannot be said to have made a major impact. I do not know why it is harder to stop government expenditures of this sort than the other kinds of government activity, but I suspect the problem is simply that from the standpoint of the citizens of California, the project is in fact a good one.[7] Their efforts were very largely concentrated in California. The cost, on the other hand, was very largely borne outside of California. There has been relatively little in the way of efforts on the part of economists to stop locally financed expenditures where I think they could have more impact. In making attacks on local expenditures, I think it is wise to keep in mind that in many cases the money actually is federal. It is not unwise of the local government to accept a gift from the national government even if the gift is not in optimal form. The conclusion that can be drawn is that rent-seeking can most often be stopped if the groups that are bearing the cost can be informed.

Turning to the other two categories, entry restriction and price control, most of these are state and local regulations, although there are, of course, federal examples. At these lower levels of government the beneficiaries and the injured groups are somewhat closer together and informing the injured group is somewhat easier. Further, an individual's activities are more likely to have effect in such a restricted area, and last but not least, most of these projects are fairly simple. Thus, it seems better to concentrate anti-rent-seeking activities in these areas.

Let us begin with the cases in which the prices are fixed by some government board, with a maximum and minimum price. This is essentially the British Columbia Egg Board, and there is a simple argument to be used against it, which is that there should be no minimum price. Consumers can hardly be protected by a minimum price. If you can get the minimum price out, the pressure group that set the thing up in the first place will probably see to it that the maximum price is eliminated.

At this point, I should perhaps mention the standard rationaliz-ation,[8] that advocates of the minimum price will almost certainly use. They will allege that if the minimum price is not imposed then some company with a lot of money will cut prices, drive the competition out of business, and then exploit its monopoly. This argument is eliminated by not arguing against the maximum price, and instead leaving that to the regular political process. The lesson here is a simple one: the best economic reasoning is not always (indeed, it is generally not) the best politics. Policy economists must formulate arguments that are most liable to lead to the desired outcome, not that are most elegant.

Restrictions on entry are subject to a variety of forms of argument. The formal rationalization – that is, that they make certain that the service provided is on a certain level of quality – can be countered by Milton Friedman's "certification," which is that the state or local government could provide certificates of competence to anyone who passed their regulations, but not prohibit people who do not have such certificates from practicing provided that there was no fraud. In other words, the person without a certificate could not tell people who solicited his services that he had one. This procedure would probably eliminate most of the monopoly gains and convert the present arrangements into something that might even be socially desirable.

The usual argument against this, of course, is that people are not bright enough even to look at the certificate. (Why people who argue this way think that people are bright enough to vote, I don't know, but they do.) To counter this argument one can move to a second line of defense, by pointing out that these regulations are not and, in fact, make very little effort to pretend to be, efforts to raise the quality of services.

Uniformly, when such restrictions are put on, everyone now in the trade is grandfathered in. Indeed, that is the reason they are put on — the current people in the trade want to have their lifetime income raised by reducing competition. Clearly, if everybody now in the trade is competent without investigation of any sort, it is unlikely that an investigation is of any use. Thus, all new proposals of this sort can be opposed quite readily.

If we turn to the older ones, there may well be an examination, usually an irrelevant examination, but the examination is given only to new entrants. The appropriate argument here is simply that it is possible for a person practicing, whether as a doctor or as a plumber, to fail to keep up with new developments. Forget old developments, or, for that matter, become a dipsomaniac. It would be desirable, therefore, that everyone in the trade not only be examined when he enters but be reexamined from time to time. It is hard to think of any argument against this, but it clearly would eliminate the political pressure for the restriction if the restriction had to take the form of continuing examinations.

Finally, there is a constitutional argument. The Supreme Court has held that requiring a waiting period for a new entrant into a state before he can go on relief violates his constitutional rights to travel freely. Prohibiting him from practicing his trade as a carpenter would also do so. Of course, if the restriction were literally evenhanded — that is, if the New York restriction on carpentry is the same for New Yorkers as for Californians who want to migrate to New York, then this constitutional argument would not exist. Such a restriction, however, would imply that if all people who are practicing carpentry in New York at the time the law was passed are admitted without examination, people who are practicing carpentry in other states at that time should also be admitted without examination. If we could get the Supreme Court to hold that this is what the Constitution said, we could feel confident that there would be absolutely no political effort to establish new restrictions on entry in the states and local governments throughout the United States.

If an examination for carpenters has been in existence for a long time so that there are not very many carpenters from other states who were carpenters at the time that the original carpenters were grandfathered in, there is a somewhat more difficult constitutional problem. Here, however, an argument would be needed that the examination is not really intended to certify people's ability as carpenters but to prevent migration from other states. It seems to me that the simple fact that the examination is not given regularly to people who are already practicing in order to make certain that they are retaining their skills, and not becoming dipsomaniacs, would be adequate here. Such constitutional arguments may or may not be successful in the courts. I recommend its use in economic arguments, even though it is not strictly relevant, simply because I think it will have a persuasive effect on the average voter.

In making any anti-rent-seeking argument, one should always point out that the data are inadequate (one can also imply in a tactful manner, that the reason that the data are inadequate is that the guilty are concealing or keeping secret evidence of their guilt). More data are always needed and generally the pressure group is to some extent unwilling to provide data because it fears strengthening your argument. Mainly, however, this argument places you in a very good position for rebuttal. Almost certainly, the pressure group representatives will argue that you are simply ignorant in their field. A response in which you say that your ignorance is partly because they are keeping secrets and ask them to provide further information generally would be helpful. In the unlikely event that they do provide additional information, of course, you have opportunity for further and better research.

A second argument that inevitably can be made is that the pressure group has something material to gain from its activities. Although we, as economists, do not regard this as in any way discreditable, the average person does. In fact, the pressure group will normally be arguing that its existence benefits people it in fact injures, but they will normally not deny that its own members are gaining, too. You will thus merely be giving strong emphasis to something the pressure group tends to pass over lightly.

If individual economists would select some blatantly undesirable activity, preferably of a state or local government, and become a modest expert on it, it is my contention that the economy would improve. Doing so does not involve a major investment. In general, these programs are not complicated, but nevertheless becoming an expert will involve some work. After becoming an expert, the economist should attempt to get media publicity for the position with the result first, of certainly attracting the attention of the pressure group, which may or may not be useful, and, second, if the economist pushes hard enough and is persistent, he probably will have at least some effect on the activity of the pressure group.

Here, I should emphasize that though I am suggesting this as an individual effort, there is no reason why small collectives of economists should not be involved, and there is certainly no reason why you should not seek out the support of other groups. The League of Women Voters, for example, tends to go about looking for good causes and you may be able to improve their taste. There are also various business groups, Rotary Clubs, and so on that are always on the lookout for a lecturer and that would give you an opportunity to provide some influence.

Persistence will, however, be necessary. The pressure group will continue and a mere couple of months' noise about it is helpful but unlikely to accomplish a great deal. Persistence is not difficult, however. Once you have passed the threshold of knowing enough about the organization so that you can regard yourself as a modest expert, it is very easy to keep up with further developments and incorporate additional data into your analyses. Further, your contacts with the media are apt to be self-reinforcing. After you have convinced people that you know a great deal about, let us say, controls on egg production, you are likely to find television program directors asking you questions about all economic matters. You should answer them, of course, to the best of your ability, and this will not only, we hope, contribute to the economic information of the public but also give media representatives an idea of your expertise so that when you bring up the subject of eggs or whatever it is, they are likely to pay attention.

Most economists only occasionally give lectures to something like the Rotary Club. I am suggesting that this aspect of professional life be sharply increased. Furthermore, I am suggesting that you become an expert on some rather obscure topic instead of giving your lecture to the Rotary Club on what is right or what is wrong with Reaganomics. This is indeed a change from the normal academic life but not a gigantic one. I am not suggesting that you devote immense amounts of time to these joint projects, merely that you do indeed devote some time to them. In a way it may be a pleasant change from the more profound and difficult work that I am sure mainly occupies your time.

So far I have been telling you how you can do good and have not explained why I think you can also do well. The first thing to be said is that of course the kind of research I am proposing does have some potential for publication in the regular economic literature. The *Journal of Law and Economics*, the *Journal of Political Economy*, *Public Policy*, and others all are interested in such articles. I would also suggest that the political science journals would be interested, although it would be necessary to make a few changes in your approach if you submitted articles to them.

But while all of these people would be interested and, I think, the prospects for publication are quite good, it has to be said that if a great many economists began working in this area it would rapidly exhaust the desire for such articles in these journals. After a while, only the very best of such articles could be published there. Further, in this case "best" would not refer entirely to the quality of the work but also to the importance of the subject matter. A new twist in cartel economics would, for example, probably be publishable when hundreds of studies of specific cartels would not.

So far, of course, the tolerance of these journals for this kind of article has by no means been exhausted and those of you who get in first could no doubt take advantage of that tolerance. Once we turn from this kind of journal publication, however, there are a number of other places with gradually decreasing prestige where you can get published. There is now a chain of economic institutes who are in general interested in studies of this kind of cartel.[9] The Borcherding and Dorosh pamphlet is a good example. Clearly this is a perfectly suitable publication to put on your vitae even if it does not carry quite so much weight as publication in the *Journal of Political Economy*. I, as a matter of fact, have three such things on my own vitae. Indeed, I would imagine that in cost–benefit terms these things are considerably more highly paying than *JPE* articles because although the payoff is not as high, the cost of producing them is also low.

Below that level there is the possibility of fairly widespread publication in such things as articles in local newspapers, letters to the editor, and so on. These are not great publications and you might want to indicate on your bibliography that you think they are not. For example, you could have a separate section for newspaper articles and letters to the editor. You might even mention your appearances on TV in this separate section.

With respect to these less important articles, speeches, and the like, the payoff in academic life is, of course, quite low per unit. Most universities, however, regard activity in the public arena as meritorious and pay it off in higher wages. It also carries with it the advertising value that an article in the *Journal of Political Economy* carries, although, once again, at a lower level.

But although these are less important publications, their cost is also quite low. Once you have become an expert in this area you could grind them out practically at will, producing a letter to the editor, for example, in a half hour. Thus, once again, the cost–benefit analysis from a pure career standpoint seems to be positive.

But this may immediately raise a question in your mind. How do I know that better information is likely to cause the end of these special-interest arrangements? After all, they have been in existence a long time and most economists know about them in general even if the public does not. They do not seem to be very secretive. I believe that they depend on either ignorance or misinformation on the part of the public. My reasons for believing so are two: first, if you discuss any of them with average voters it will turn out that they have never heard of them, or if they have heard of them, they are badly misinformed about them. In the case of the British Columbia Egg Board, the average voter probably does not know that there is such an organization. The voter who does probably has bought the argument that the organization stabilizes prices and protects the family farm.

But in addition to this informal public opinion poll, there is another and, in my opinion, more important reason. If we think of the British Columbia Egg Board, any economist could quickly arrange a set of taxes on eggs together with direct subsidies to the people who were in the business of producing eggs[10] that would make both the customers and the producers of the eggs better off. We do not see this direct subsidy being used. Why do pressure groups not simply aim at a low tax on the entire population that is used to pay a direct sum of money to them rather than these clearly non-Pareto-optimal arrangements that we in fact observe? I think the only available explanation for this is that they know that a certain amount of confusion and misdirection is necessary. A direct cash transfer, a tax of $10 per family in British Columbia for the purpose of paying a pension to the 300 people who happen to own egg factories at the time the program was put into effect, would never go through because it is too blatant and obvious. It is necessary that these things be covered by some kind of deception. Granted that I am right about this – that these programs require that the people be misinformed – informing them is likely to terminate the program. No politician is going to tax all of his constituents a small sum of money in order to give a large sum of money to a small group no matter how well organized that small group is if everyone knows that is what he is doing. Economists can see to it that they do know.

Note here, also that the nature of the mass media is on your side. The mass media all aim at large audiences. The small pressure group does not have much chance of getting the attention of the mass media except, possibly, unfavorable attention. The small pressure group very likely has its own journal, which it uses for internal communication, but the owner of a TV station or a newspaper will tend to come down for his customers en masse, not a tiny minority of his customers. Thus, not only is secrecy and deception necessary here but the nature of the mass media means that unmasking of these villains is likely to be popular with those who want to make money in the media business.

I am sure all of this sounds rather wild to most of you. I gave an earlier version of this paper at my own university and a young ABD, who had been listening and apparently could not believe his ears came up afterward and asked me whether it was really true that I was suggesting that he not only study up on some local government-managed cartel but seek publication in places other than the *JPE*. I assumed him that was my objective. He went away looking astounded, not, I think, at the brilliance of my ideas, but at the eccentricity.

This particular young man will, I think, have great difficulty getting any publications ever in the *JPE*. Competition is stiff (even to this day I have about half of my submissions turned down[11]), and most economists will never get a single article published in a leading journal. Still, I assume all of you are members of that small minority who do occasionally break into print in such places as *JPE*, the *AER*, and the *QJE*.

Turning to the problem of the man who does have great difficulty getting anything published, something on his vitae is better than nothing, and the proposal that I am making is a way in which he can pretty much guarantee he will have at least something on his vitae. For the more productive economist, who does currently produce articles for the leading journals, it is still helpful to add additional items even if these additional items are not of Nobel Prize quality. Once again, the cost of producing these things is comparatively low, so you make a good deal per unit of effort.

Even if there were no beneficial impact on your career, nevertheless, I would urge it on you. All of us are, to some minor extent, charitable and this is a particularly convenient way for economists to work out their charitable feelings. Getting rid of the Brtitish Columbia Egg Board might not impress you as a major accomplishment, but individuals can expect to have only small impacts on the massive structure that we call modern society. It is likely that you will do more good for the world by concentrating on abolishing some such organization in your locality than the average person does – indeed, very much more. It is an unusual form of charity, but a form in which the payoff would be high. But although such work falls squarely in the path of virtue, it also has positive payoffs. You can, to repeat my title, do well while you are doing good.

Notes

Notes to chapter 1

1 See Julius Margolis, "The Economic Evaluation of Federal Water Resource Development," *American Economic Review*, 49 (March, 1959), 69–111, for a review of some of the recent literature on the subject.

2 Pioneers have begun to appear. See Anthony Downs, *An Economic Theory of Democracy* (New York: Harper & Bros., 1957), and Duncan Black, *The Theory of Committees and Elections* (Cambridge: Cambridge University Press, 1958).

3 See Black, (*Committees and Elections*, for a comprehensive view of the difficulties discovered to date.

4 This problem is discussed in a paper presented by Julius Margolis before the Conference on Public Finances: Needs, Sources, and Utilization, of the Universities – National Bureau of Economic Research Committee, held April 10 and 11, 1959, at Charlottesville, Virginia.

5 In practice the problem of getting the unanimous agreement of 51 persons might be insoluble. Since we are now only discussing a rather unlikely special case, we can ignore the point. Alternatively, the reader can assume that there are 53 or 54 maximizers, and those who set their terms too high can simply be left out.

6 In the "Theory of the Reluctant Duelist" (*American Economic Review*, 46 [December, 1956], 909–23) Daniel Ellsberg contends that game theory really only applies to "reluctant" players. Our case is a particularly pure example. The voter must "play the game" by entering into bargains with 50 of his fellows, even though this leads to rather unsatisfactory results, simply because any other course of action is even worse.

7 The fact that he is taxed for other roads not part of his bargain reduces his real income and hence, to some extent, reduces the amount of road repairing he would wish to consume.

8 James Buchanan kindly permitted me to present this paper before his graduate seminar in public finance, and the objections made by some of the students tended to follow these lines.

9 Not necessarily for all. There might well be one or more farmers whose personal preference schedules called for a large enough investment in roads so that the "maximizing equilibrium" was preferable to the "Kantian median."

10 "Problems of Majority Voting," *Journal of Political Economy*, 67 (December, 1959), 571–9. Throughout this article the term "majority" is equivalent to "simple majority" unless otherwise stated. Both these terms refer to the nearest whole number of voters over 50 percent of those voting in any election under consideration. I am grateful to Professor Tullock for reading the first draft of this criticism; his comments have resulted in the elimination of several errors from the final version.

11 In some American communities – particularly in California – voters do vote directly on a large number of specific proposals for expenditure. However, few of these proposals are of the type exemplified by Tullock's model, in which expenditures benefit individual voters directly. Most of the proposals which voters pass upon benefit very few voters directly, except for occasional neighborhood-improvement effects. Spending on such projects as jails, mental hospitals, and other state institutions must, for most voters, be judged on the basis of whether the benefits to the *community as a whole* justify additional tax burdens which they *personally* will bear. This involves a different kind of judgment from that discussed by Tullock. Thus, even though too many citizens vote to make logrolling possible, such expenditure bills are often passed.

12 The discrimination assumption is not operative in cases where taxes are aimed at specific groups, such as a special assessment to pay for a local street.

13 In some cases citizens do vote directly upon individual legislative acts, as described in n. 2. However, even in these cases the acts voted upon comprise only a small fraction of all the acts considered by the legislature, and citizens cannot bargain directly with each other because the number of voters is too large. Thus Tullock's model – which is based upon personal bargaining and vote-trading among individual voters – does not accurately describe even those few parts

of the world in which direct referendums play a significant role in expenditure decision-making.

14 Gordon Tullock, *A Preliminary Investigation of the Theory of Constitutions* (Department of International Studies, University of South Carolina, 1959). (Mimeographed.)

15 However, this outcome is extremely unlikely because of the secret ballot. Since no legislator can be positive who voted for him and who voted against him, he must spread the benefits of his policies over all citizens in his district who might have been responsible for getting him elected. Only if he has been supported by a personally identifiable bloc of 51 percent of his constituents can he afford to ignore the other 49 percent – and even in that case the need to "take out a little insurance" would probably prompt him to benefit a few more citizens just in case some members of his supporting bloc defected. Thus, even if 51 percent of the legislators form a solid bloc in the legislature, where open voting is the rule, the benefits of their policies will be spread over many more than 26 percent of all the voters – up to as many as 51 percent. I am indebted to James Q. Wilson of the University of Chicago for pointing out this fact.

16 If each does accept his defeat as certain, he loses all motivation for furthering the interests of his constituents. Instead he will exploit his office – while it lasts – purely for personal gain (which may take the form of pride in excellent statesmanship as well as financial prosperity). In this case the basic structure of the representative system breaks down, since the representatives have no motive for acting in the interests of those who elect them.

17 A third outcome is possible – the one described in n. 16. This outcome is the only one consistent with Tullock's generalized conclusions, but it is self-contradictory in the long run. If elected representives in some areas always face certain defeat when running for re-election, they will abandon their function as representatives of their constituents. In this case the constituents will not long tolerate continued operation of democracy or continued membership in this geographical grouping. Either they will agitate for a dictatorship or some other non-democratic system which gives more weight to their interests, or they will attempt to secede from that particular democracy and set up another one in which their interests will be better served. Thus, the model which supports Tullock's conclusions also implies internal conflict which will tend to destroy the political society it posits.

18 Even under unanimous role, vote-trading would still occur. Since

every individual would have power of veto over every bill, each could "blackmail" any majority which wanted to pass a bill by threatening to withdraw his vote unless some bill he wanted was also passed. The impossibility of creating 100 percent cartels because of this constant threat of "blackmail" is what makes unanimous rule so impractical.

19 This argument is presented in Anthony Downs, "Why the Government Budget is Too Small in a Democracy," *World Politics*, 12 (July, 1960), 541–63.

20 Tullock, "Problems," and *A Preliminary Investigation of the Theory of Constitutions* (an 83-page draft which was circulated in hectograph form to a few scholars, including Downs).

21 See "Problems," p. 00 last paragraph.

22 Again I can accept Downs's description of the model for the purposes of this discussion, with one exception. He states that the legislators "stand for elections 'on their records.'" Perhaps my presentation of the matter was rather ambiguous, but the candidates run on a combination of promises for the future and their record for keeping such promises in the past. The matter would be of little importance were it not for the fact that James Q. Wilson gave Downs a criticism of the model based on this misinterpretation.

23 In considering the real-world relevance of the model, the emphasis should be put upon the capability. We have national parties, but they seldom exercise effective control over such matters as the rivers and harbors appropriation.

24 P. 00. In "Problems," I am discussing a model of direct democracy while Downs is discussing the more complicated system with a legislative assembly, but for this issue the two systems do not differ.

25 Some of the necessary additional models are presented in Tullock, *A Preliminary Investigation*. More will appear in *The Calculus of Consent* (Ann Arbor: University of Michigan Press), a much enlarged and improved discussion of democracy, written jointly by James Buchanan and myself. Even this book does not pretend to be a complete theory of democracy, but only a preliminary analysis.

26 Anthony Downs, "Why the Government Budget is Too Small."

27 See Black *Committees and Elections*; Kenneth J. Arrow, *Social Choice and Individual Values* (New York: John Wiley & Sons, 1951); and Anthony downs, *An Economic Theory of Democracy*, pp. 60–2.

28 Tullock, *The Calculus of Consent* will contain a method of avoiding the problem. The evasion, however, is based on the logrolling model to which Downs takes exception.

Notes to chapter 2

This paper was presented by the author, Professor of International Studies at University of South Carolina, to the Third Congress of the Southern Economic Association (Atlanta, Georgia, November, 1960).

1 The only economists to whom it will not be new will be those who have seen the mimeographed version of *The Calculus of Consent* (James Buchanan and Gordon Tullock, University of Michigan Press). Although this article is not directly drawn from the book, it follows the same general line of reasoning and is intended as a sort of introduction to this new field.

2 The relationship between this model and the one I introduced on p. 11 of my article, "Problems of Majority Voting" *Journal of Political Economy* (December, 1959, 571–9) is obviously close. The "Problems" model, in fact, is a single point on the continuum to be introduced on the next few pages.

3 Costs associated with shifting some activity from the private sector to the public are, of course, frequently discussed by economists. These costs, however, have normally been essentially the bureaucratic costs of administration, not the intrinsic costs of the decisions themselves. For a partial exception, see Friedrich A. von Hayek, "Free Enterprise and Competitive Order," *Individualism and Economic Order* (Chicago, 1948), 107–18.

4 Tullock, "Problems," pp. 571–9. See also Dr Anthony Downs's comment, "In Defense of Majority Voting," in the February 1961 issue (p. 192) and my "Reply to a Traditionalist," in the February 1961 issue (p. 200).

5 See Paul A. Samuelson "The Pure Theory of Public Expenditures," *Review of Economics and Statistics* (1954), 387.

6 See Richard A. Musgrave's *The Theory of Public Finance* for the most developed treatment of the problem in the traditional system.

7 Strictly speaking, this is only true for the whole series of decisions on road repairing. Since our model provides that each individual road-repair project be voted on separately and since such a project directly helps only those living along that particular road, costs and benefits do not match for each individual on each project. It is only when we consider road repairing in general that the margins match.

8 For a comprehensive discussion of the work so far done in this field, see Tullock, *The Calculus of Consent*.

Notes to chapter 3

1   Given the title of my paper it would have been impossible for me to conceal the political basis of the problem. In private conversations with several economists I have presented the problem in much the same terms as the next few pages but without giving them any idea of the "industry" under consideration. They have normally accepted the argument and the solution I propose on purely economic grounds. Thus it is experimentally established that the problem can be solved in economic terms even though it arises in political systems.

2   The analogous problem in economics has received considerable attention recently. Perhaps the best discussion is in Joe S. Bain, *Barriers to New Competition* (Harvard, 1959). More recent work has included William H. Martin, "Potential Competition and the United States Chlorine-Alkali Industry," *Journal of Industrial Economics* (July 1961); Elizabeth Brunner, "A Note on Potential Competition," *Journal of Industrial Economics* (July, 1961); Franco Modigliani, "New Developments on the Oligopoly Front," *Journal of Political Economy* (June, 1958).

3   It is not, of course, necessarily impractical for small parts of the government. The government itself must be chosen by the voters, but it might contract for the performance of various services by the method we are here discussing and obtain qualified experts to judge the bids.

4   If another voting rule is actually used, then analogous problems arise.

5   The United States has had one of the parties disintegrate, with a temporary cessation of organized potential competition three times: the "era of good feeling," the period just before the foundation of the Republican Party, and in 1872 when the Democrats did not nominate an independent presidential candidate.

6   It might be argued that the communities – and there are many of them – which are governed by such a system are not really democratic. The council is not really subject to any check unless it does something really awful. The councilmen's principle satisfaction comes from "doing their duty." If this theory is true, they would be compelled to give good government, according to their own lights, in order to get the satisfaction for which they hold the office. The system would really be aristocratic government with *noblesse oblige* as the operative motive.

7   In Switzerland and a few other places this compensation is purely nonpecuniary.

Notes to chapter 4

1 I regret to say that the phantom has stalked my classrooms with particular vigor. I hereby apologize to my students for inflicting it upon them.

2 The situation with complete independence of preferences is discussed in C. D. Campbell and G. Tullock, "A Measure of the Importance of Cyclical Majorities," *The Economic Journal*, 75 (December, 1965), 853–7.

3 Kenneth J. Arrow, *Social Choice and Individual Values*, rev. edn (New York: John Wiley, 1963).

4 Arrow, *Social Choice*, p. 74–91.

5 See Duncan Black, "On the Rationale of Group Decision-Making," *Journal of Political Economy*, 56 (February 1948), 23–4, and *The Theory of Committees and Elections* (Cambridge University Press, 1958), for fuller discussion of single-peaked curves.

6 R. A. Newing and Duncan BLack, *Committee Decisions with Complementary Valuation* (London: William Hodge, 1951).

7 Arrow, *Social Choice*, pp. 51–9.

8 Usually the limitations on the introduction of trival amendments is not this formal, but it normally will be impossible to make very small changes in money bills.

9 Strictly speaking there would be an indifference point when the perpendicular bisector ran directly through the point of maximum preference for one voter. At this point the vote would stand: for *A*, 499,999, for the alternative, 499,999, indifferent, 1.

10 The referee suggested that the last two paragraphs be replaced by the following passage: "Suppose that two points, *A* and *B*, are equidistant from the center but that *no one's optimum lies exactly on their perpendicular bisector*. Therefore one, say *A*, is preferred to the other. All points within a small neighborhood of *A* are preferred to *B*, and some among these will be further from the center than *B* is." A little experimentation on the understandability of both my version and his seems to show that some people find one easier to follow and some the other. Including both, therefore, seems sensible.

11 If there were some body or person who had control of the order in which proposals are offered for vote, and if that body or person had perfect knowledge of the preferences of the voters, then by proper choice of alternatives it would be possible for the "Rules Committee" to arrange the vote in such a way as to lead to substantially any outcome it wished. See Benjamin Ward, "Majority Rule and

Allocation," *Journal of Conflict Resolution* (1961), 379–89.

12 For a proof of the normal absence of majority motion under assumptions like those we are here using see Newing and Black, *Committee Decisions*, pp. 21–3.

13 Black, *Committees and elections*.

14 Occasional cases which appear to involve cycles have been discovered. See William Riker, "Arrow's Theorem and Some Examples of the Paradox of Voting," in *Mathematical Applications in Political Science*, S. Sidney Ulmer, Harold Guetzkow, and William Riker (eds) (Dallas, Texas: Arnold Foundation, Southern Methodist University, 1965), 41–60.

15 Most rules of procedure have such provisions, but they are usually easy to avoid if a majority favors the measure which is reintroduced.

16 If they differ in only one characteristic, then the work of Duncan Black indicates that the cyclical majority is most unlikely.

17 Circles in two dimensional issue space. When more than two variables are considered, the issue space would have more than two dimensions and the indifference hypersurfaces would be hyperspheres.

18 In a very kind letter Professor Arrow generally agreed with the argument presented in this paper. However, he pointed out that the following portion is not mathematically strict. He expressed a desire for "a stronger and stricter statement." I also would like to convert what is now a strong argument into a mathematical proof, but have been unable to do so. Perhaps some reader with greater facility in the use of mathematical tools will be able to repair the deficiency.

19 Even with large numbers of individuals a combination of certain strong symmetry relations between their preference curves and special arrangements of their optima will lead to significant cycles. The only cases I have been able to develop involve very unrealistic shapes for the indifference curves and there seems no point in presenting them here.

Notes to chapter 5

1 Sometimes informal pressures can function very much like a government. As a general rule, however, human experience seems to indicate that informal pressure is not sufficient and we normally use governmental pressure in such cases.

2 Cf. Duncan Black, *The Theory of Committees and Elections* (Cambridge, 1958).

Notes to chapter 6

1 Harold Hotelling, "Stability in Competition," *Economic Journal*, 39 (March, 1929), 41–57; Duncan Black, "On the Rationale of Group Decision Making," *Journal of Political Economy*, 56 (February, 1948), 23–34; Anthony Downs, *An Economic Theory of Democracy* (New York, 1957).

2 Duncan Black, *A Theory of Committees and Elections* (Cambridge, 1958); Otto A. Davis and M. J. Hinich, "A Mathematical Model of Policy Formation in a Democratic Society," in *Mathematical Applications in Political Science*, II, J. Bernd (ed.) (Dallas, 1966); Davis and Hinich, "Some Results Related to a Mathematical Model of Policy Formation in a Democratic Society," in *Mathematical Applications in Political Science*, III, J. Bernd (ed.) (Charlottesville, 1967); Davis and Hinich, "On the Power and Importance of the Mean Preference in a Mathematical Model of Democratic Choice," *Public Choice*, 5 (Fall, 1968), 59–72; Gordon Tullock, *Toward a Mathematics of Politics* (Ann Arbor, 1966).

3 See James M. Buchanan and Gordon Tullock, *The Calculus of Consent* (Ann Arbor, 1962).

4 See Davis and Hinich, "On the Power and Importance of the Mean Preference," p. 68; Tullock, *Toward a Mathematics of Politics*, pp. 57–61.

5 For an application of this process see Colin Campbell and Gordon Tullock, "A Measure of the Importance of Cyclical Majorities," *Economic Journal*, 78 (Dec. 1967) 853–75.

6 For a demonstration see Kenneth Arrow, "Tullock and an Existence Theorem," *Public Choice*, 6 (Spring, 1969), 105–11.

7 This does not mean that their optima or intensities are the same as Mr A's, but simply that all of their indifference curves would have the same general shape as Mr A's.

8 A modern theory of bargaining can be said to have been initiated by J. von Neumann and O. Morgenstern in their *Theory of Genes and Economic Behavior* (Princeton, 1944). For a summary of developments since publication of *Theory of Games and Economic Behavior* and some interesting experimental results in a three-person situation, see William Riker, "Bargaining in a Three Person Game," *American Political Science Review*, 61 (September, 1967), 642–56.

9 The assumption of equal division is not strictly necessary for the general conclusions reached below. The equations would also be

solvable for other assumptions as to the division of the spoils between the members of the logrolling bargain.

10 The derivation of these results is simple but not obvious. Since A is equal to B, and C is equal to 0, the first equation in table 6.1 reduces to: $L_A^2 = 6A^2 - 100A + 500$. Differentiating (the variable L_A^2 with respect to A) and setting the differential equal to 0 produces a value of A equal to 8.33 which minimizes both L_A^2 and L_a. Substitution of this value into the equations of table 6.1 gives the numbers shown. Similar methods are used for all further computations in this article. The computations were carried out on a slide rule, which is rather unusual in these days of computers, and hence there is a possibility of error in the final decimal.

11 See James Coleman, "The Possibility of a Social Welfare Function," *American Economic Review*, 56 (December, 1966), 1105–22, for a discussion of this point. His article led to comments by R. E. Park and Dennis C. Mueller which, together with a reply by Coleman, are printed in the December 1967 issue of the *American Economic Review*, pp. 1300–16.

12 The simplest way of understanding this problem is to assume that an individual purchases other peoples' votes with his own. There is no obvious reason, if there are more than three voters, why the votes purchased by Mr A should be the same votes as those purchased by say, Mr C, although Mr A's collection of purchases includes Mr C's vote and Mr C's collection of purchases includes Mr A's vote. Mr A could, for example, make up his majority in a five-person voting system out of A, B, and C, and Mr C make up his out of C, D, and E. Mr E, similarly, might have a majority which consists of C and B as well as himself.

13 The proportional representation system used so much on the continent of Europe generally speaking makes it impossible for less than the majority of the voters to have the influence shown. In Anglo-Saxon countries, however, the possibility does exist for the minority of voters obtaining the type of profits shown here.

14 Davis and Hinich, "A Mathematical Model," "Some Results," and "On the Power and Importance of the Mean Preference;" Tullock, *Toward a Mathematics of Politics*.

15 William Riker, *The Theory of Political Coalitions* (New Haven, 1962).

Notes to chapter 7

1 William A. Niskanen, *Bureaucracy and Representative Government* (Chicago: Aldine-Atherton, 1971).

Notes to chapter 8

This article was much improved by comments from T. Nicolaus Tideman.

1 Duncan Black, *The Theory of Committees and Elections* (Cambridge, 1958), 137–9.

2 Gordon Tullock, "The General Irrelevance of the General Impossibility Theorem," *Quarterly Journal of Economics*, 81 (May, 1967); this paper also appeared in the paperback edition of Tullock, *Toward a Mathematics of Politics* (Ann Arbor, 1972), and page citations throughout this chapter are to the 1972 edition.

3 R. McKelvey, *General Conditions for Global Informal Voting Models: Some Implications for Agenda Control* (SUPA, Carnegie–Mellon University). (Mimeographed.)

4 Tullock, "The General Irrelevance," p. 31. Also see p. 34, "there are numerous positions outside the Pareto optimal area which can get majority over areas within it;" p. 43 "Thus it is possible, by a simple majority vote, to reach points at almost any portion of the issue space."

5 I don't propose to run over the argument itself because it is fairly lengthy and already available in print in two different places.

6 Some careless discussion of this point implies that this process could lead to a point outside the Paretian area. The agenda controller has no motive to go anywhere except his own optimum and his own optimum is by definition in the Pareto optimal area. Only through accident can the outcome be outside the Paretian area.

7 There is, of course, some probability, roughly equivalent to the probability that all the molecules of air in the room in which you are sitting will accumulate in one corner, that by sheer accident the motions offered will be such as to lead to a conclusion well away from the center.

8 Gordon Tullock, "A Simple Algebraic Logrolling Model," *American Economic Review*, 60 (June, 1970), 419–26; the table appears on p. 423 [p. 000 in this volume] as table 2.

9 Calculation methods for these numbers are contained in the original article.

10 James M. Buchanan and Gordon Tullock, *The Calculus of Consent* (Ann Arbor, 1962); Gordon Tullock, *Entrepreneurial Politics*, Research Monograph No. 5 (University of Virginia, 1962).

11 See T. N. Tideman and Gordon Tullock, "A New and Superior Process for Making Social Choices," *Journal of Political Economy* (October, 1976), 1145–59.

12 Buchanan and Tullock, *The Calculus of Consent*, p. 149.

13 J. von Neumann and O. Morgenstern, *Theory of Games and Economic Behavior*, 3rd edn (Princeton University Press, 1953); Buchanan and Tullock, *The Calculus of Consent*, ibid.

14 If cash side payments were permitted, this situation would not be stable. Cash side payments are, however, prohibited by almost all voting systems. I feel this prohibition is wise but will not go into the subject here.

15 Tullock, *Toward a Mathematics of Politics*, pp. 100–43.

16 H. Butler, "An Analysis of the Distribution of Federal Expenditures by Congressional Districts" (University of Miami, 1980). (Unpublished.)

17 J. T. Bennett and E. R. Mayberry, "Federal Tax Burdens and Grant Benefits to States: the Impact of Imperfect Representation" (George Mason University, Va., n.d.). (Unpublished.)

18 Charles R. Plott, "Some Organizational Influences on Urban Renewal Decisions," *American Economic Review*, 58 (May, 1968), 306–21.

19 For the most recent work in this field see B. A. Ray, "Federal Spending and the Selection of Committee Assignments in the US House of Representatives," *American Journal of Political Science*, 24 (1980), 494–510.

20 David Klingaman, "A Note on a Cyclical Majority Problem," *Public Choice*, 6 (Sprng, 1969), 99–101.

21 J. A. Ferejohn, *Pork Barrel Politics* (Stanford University Press, 1974).

22 For an argument on the other side see K. A. Shepsle and B. R. Weingast, *Political Preferences for the Pork Barrel: a Generalization*, Working Paper No. 57 (Washington University, June 1980).

23 With a purely redistributive context one would expect to be purely egalitarian, but granted the kind of acts that Congress actually passes, rough egalitarianism is all that can be expected.

24 S. J. Brams and W. Riker, "Models of Coalition Formation in Voting Bodies," in *Mathematical Applications in Political Science*, VI (Charlottesville, 1972), 79–124.

25 I was mildly involved myself in rather similar negotiations between the American government and President Rhee of Korea.

26 This does not seem to be true in the United States. Butler, "An Analysis" shows that marginal constituencies get no more in government projects than safe ones. Apparently, in the American Congress a vote is a vote is a vote.

27 Here, of course, I am assuming fairly good information. Assuming realistic information conditions, cost can be a very large multiple of the benefit rather than the simple two to one level which I have described here.

28 Since the election of President Carter the rivers and harbors bill, as a whole, has had considerable difficulty and it is possible that eventually this particular bit of pork will disappear.

Notes to chapter 9

1 At the time this paper was written, the new President of Mexico had, as Minister of Interior, ordered police to fire on demonstrating students, killing 428. The Mexican government, although it somehow succeeds in concealing its nature, is in fact a rather unusual serial dictatorship, with the dictator changed every six years. It is more notable for corruption and general inefficiency than for direct oppression.

2 There is, of course, also the possibility of fines, but fines in general cannot be used against people who refuse to pay them unless you threaten them with some alternative.

3 Arabic would be almost as good.

4 See Gordon Tullock, *Trials on Trial* (University of Columbia Press, 1981).

5 It should be pointed out that there is no intrinsic reason why a trusted attorney cannot be permitted to cross-examine these witnesses, etc. The problem is preventing the defendant from finding out who they are, not from preventing a respectable member of the bar from finding out who they are.

Notes to chapter 10

1 In a special sense one could say almost all welfare programs in Western countries are of this type since by any realistic bookkeeping,

citizenship in the United States, France, etc. is the largest single asset held by the average such citizen, and people who do not have that asset (worth probably in excess of $100,000) are barred from these programs. Since most of the poor people in the world are poor specifically because they do not have that particular asset, i.e, citizenship in a developed country, we could say that substantially all existing aid programs in Western countries have a negative wealth test: you have to have something worth about $100,000 before you become eligible for payments.

    Although this subject interests me a great deal, it is not what I had been asked to write on, and hence for the rest of this essay I will be discussing income testing only when relief or services are given to citizens.

2 Indeed, the special medical faciliities for Brezhnev seem to be quite unprecedented. In his recent visit to Germany it was revealed that he is not only always accompanied by a crew of doctors, nurses, etc. but that they have a special van which is in essence a custom-designed intensive care room for his particular collection of illnesses. It was flown to West Germany in a special plane.

3 In the particular case of medicine there might be additional motives for being concerned with the medical treatment for Mr 1, due to the externalities that sometimes arise in medical matters. Since, however, I am basically interested in income-tested programs in general and am only using the medical program as a special case, I will not discuss the problem further.

4 Strictly speaking with our small group of three voters it is unlikely that Mr 1 would make this particular calculation. With millions of voters, however, this line of reasoning applies rigorously (see J. M. Buchanan, "The Inconsistencies of the National Health Service," reprinted in *Theory of Public Choice: Political Applications of Economics*, J. M. Buchanan and R. D. Tollison (eds) (Ann Arbor, 1972)).

5 The assumption that the tax structure is not changed at the same time is crucial here, but necessary if I am to discuss effect of income-tested versus universal programs. There is no doubt that by making the tax system more progressive you can benefit the poor (ignoring incentive effects). If you do that at the same time that you introduce a universal program, the benefit which the poor received from the increase in the progressivity of the tax could very well make the whole package much to the interest of the poor. They would, however, still be better off if a tax were made more progressive and income testing were retained.

6 Some people would say this might not be true because the expenditure of the additional $20 on medicine for him would be of more value to him than the $50 which they would allege he would waste on something else, like drink or the numbers game. I don't regard this as a truthful description of the behavior of the poor, but there are people who believe this.

7 C. M. Lyndsay and B. Zycher, "More Evidence on Director's Law" (University of California – Los Angeles, 1978), 3. (Unpublished.)

8 Gordon Tullock, "The Charity of the Uncharitable," *Western Economic Journal*, 9 (1971), 379–92.

9 People who actually had zero income before, if they were to stay alive must at any event have consumed food. Presumably this would be slightly more expensive because of the tax increase. But they are also, as we have noted above, likely to have their other government payments reduced or not increased as much as they otherwise would have been. Note here, that I have assumed that the net effect of the change does not involve an improvement in medical service.

10 C. Weaver, "The Emergence, Growth, and Redirection of Social Security: an Interpretive History from a Public Choice Perspective" (Virginia Polytechnic Institute and State Univerity, Blacksburg, Va, 1977). (PhD dissertation.)

11 Martin Pfaff, "Patterns of Inequality in Income: Selected Determinance, Countries, and Policy Issues for the 1980s," paper prepared for ASSA (Association of Social Science Associates) meeting.

12 Werner Pommerehne, "Public Choice Approaches to Explaining Fiscal Redistribution," paper presented at the 34th Conference of the International Institute of Public Finance, Hamburg, Germany (September, 1978).

13 L. Jagannadahm and C. M. Palvia, *Problems of Pensioners* (New Delhi: Banurha, 1978).

14 See Weaver, "The Emergence, Growth, and Redirection of Social Security."

15 Professor Irwin Garfinckle was the organizer of the conference at which the paper was presented. His general political position is certainly well to my left.

Notes to chapter 11

1 This is also an example of the lack of careful research and thought in this area. I have not bothered to go back and find the details of an article I read rather casually in a newspaper.

2 It should be said there that the price control legislation may be a misunderstood private good legislation rather than misunderstood public good legislation. It is sometimes suggested that the average individual thinks that the rise in the price of the things that he purchases are caused by inflation, while the rise in the price of whatever he sells is caused by his own virtue. Thus he may think that a fair price control system would permit his income to continue rising while stopping the prices he pays from rising. Thus he has a selfish rather than a public good motive here. I doubt that this is, in fact, the explanation, but it might be.

3 Or for that matter thought that it endangered me. The arguments are opposite but have the same relevance for this paper.

4 Not quite so hard as they did for improved pensions, of course.

5 The particular method of proportional representation used in Switzerland means that many, many members of the legisation can be unseated by really quite small changes in the preferential vote.

6 In some cases, of course, the transfer involves an essentially voluntary present from the well-off to the poor and, in this case, there are public good aspects.

7 This, by the way, is not in any sense a new phenomenon. When Jefferson first became President he found himself with the combination of a fairly large military machine and a rather difficult foreign policy situation. He decided to cut sharply on the military in spite of the difficult foreign policy situation; a decision which imposed on his successor and friend, President Madison, the disastrous war of 1812. The intriguing feature of his budget cuts on defense, however, is that although he cut back very, very sharply on the actual fighting part of the army and navy, he did not close down naval bases or arsenals. The combat part of the military was cut back but the logrolling part was not. In this, as in so many other areas, Jefferson was the founder of modern American politics.

8 Paul A. Samuelson, "The Pure Theory of Public Expenditures," *Review of Economics and Statistics*, xxxvi (November, 1954), 387–9.

Notes to chapter 12

1   The apparent reason that American airlines' prices were lower than those in Europe was not that our airlines were any less monopolistic but that they were more efficient, with the result that the optimum monopoly price for them was lower than the optimum monopoly price for such monsters of inefficiency as Air France or Japan Airlines.

2   Unfortunately, this partial deregulation seems to have stopped. (I hope temporarily.) Once again, it is encouraging that most economists were opposed to this regulation.

3   It is not that the optimal tariff literature is wrong. It is that it can be misused and that economists are more likely to have a postive effect on public policy because rent-seeking forces will be pushing for a tarriff that is far beyond any optimal tariff.

4   The booklet is *The Egg Marketing Board, A Case Study of Monopoly and Its Social Costs*, by Thomas Borcherding and Gary W. Dorosh (Vancouver: The Fraser Institute, 1981).

5   The "deregulation" that has been so successful in recent years in the United States is an example. It has become more or less a fad with most of the correspondents for the *Washington Post* who were in favor of it without having any clear idea why.

6   I leave aside here those cases in which if we look only at the short run, as unfortunately the voter does, the beneficiaries outnumber the people who pay. Price controls on gas are a current example.

7   Ignoring, of course, those particular farmers who will be damaged by the canal across the delta.

8   I encountered it in high school.

9   The bulk of them owe their origin to the energies of Antony Fisher.

10 Some of these might, of course, decide to stop producing eggs and move to Hawaii on the subsidy.

11 I have a large collection of unpublished articles.

Index

Index by Geoffrey C. Jones